TO JIM CO
" CRUISE

Broke Down,

A Million Miles From Home.

Now What?

Roger A. Jetter

12-2-2022

With Daniel E. Jetter

Drive'em

Published by BookLocker.com, Inc., St. Petersburg, Florida.

Printed on acid-free paper.

BookLocker.com, Inc.
2017

First Edition

For our great nephew, Colt Theodore James Sonnichsen, and great

nieces, Emma Grace and Kate Alisabeth Sonnichsen.

TABLE OF CONTENTS

INTRODUCTION

I first met Roger and Dan in 1976 while attending local runs and shows representing a club they belonged to called the Nifty Fifties. It didn't take long to realize these two guys believed street cars were to drive and they did – everywhere throughout Colorado and into Nebraska and Wyoming. They both went and they both drove promoting their hobby and their sport. It didn't take me long to explain the benefits of a membership into the NSRA and how they should consider building and driving street rods too.

Being street machiners with Tri-five Chevys, Roger attended the NSRA Street Machine Nats in Tulsa in 1976. Their treks together as a traveling duo began in 1977 with several local rod runs, topped by a trip to the Street Rod Nationals in St. Paul, Minnesota, and back home for more area events. All the while Roger continued to share his love of artwork through the pen name Rave Swell. A most unique name chosen by Roger as the flattery and respect he had for artist Dave Bell found him imitating Dave's unique style.

While Dan and Roger continued their roles in the Nifty Fifties, I was invited to attend their annual All Chevy Day in Denver to promote the National Street Rod Association. Knowing it was for Chevys only, I borrowed a classic Chevrolet emblem from a friend that was also attending, taping it to the headlight bar of my 32 Ford five window. It's really too bad everyone didn't think it was as funny as Dan, Roger and most of the club members did.

In May of 1978, Roger and Dan joined together with a group of Denver rodders to continue the NSRA motto of "fun with cars" and formed the Rocky Mountain Un-Club with their first official meeting to follow in June. Beginning with the announcement of this newly formed club was the soon-to-follow first edition of the "Un-News" in July, written and edited by Roger with a promise of being an introduction to the club members plus to serve as a communication to other clubs. The schedule - Published whenever they got a "round tuitt." It is that summer Roger and Dan started their long distance runs together and the stories of this book began. A journey that continues today, adding even more pages for yet another story.

The first pure street rod event of all pre-1948 rods for Roger was in August of 1978. With his newly and mostly completed 1940 Studebaker coupe making several test runs for a couple of months, Roger together with a fellow club member in his 1946 Ford coupe each grabbed a traveling companion to go along with an assortment of tools, spare parts and safety equipment and they all headed to Merced, California, for the NSRA Western Street Rod Nationals. I believe it would be safe to say they were bitten.

The first ever NSRA Appreciation Day was held in September of 1979; a day designed just for NSRA members, those wishing to join and hosted by the Colorado and Wyoming NSRA street rod and street machine representatives. Roger graciously designed, illustrated, printed and donated the flyers via Rave Swell. It was a grand day and due to all, Appreciation Days continue to be held each and every year and in all parts of the country by the NSRA Representatives.

It's been a long time since that first meeting of Dan and Roger Jetter. And a lot of things have changed in the street rodding sport, hopefully for the betterment of our hobby and sport. All while driving these street rods and street machines, meeting new and lasting friends along the way. One thing that hasn't changed and never will is "what if they break." It isn't if they will break, it is simply when, and Roger and Dan share with us some reminding stories of being "broken down a million miles from home." Then again, it doesn't matter, we built them and we still carry tools and spare parts to fix them along the roadway if need be. You have to admit, if they're not worth driving, they're not worth owning.

Thank you Dan and Roger for the great memories, the fun times and most importantly for the lasting friendship while having fun with cars.

Keep'em Street'n,
Jerry Kennedy
Special Events Director
National Street Rod Association ®

FOREWORD

No doubt the cover caught your attention. While that photo may look like it'd be somewhere in the Midwest while Dan and I were on a rod run, it is not the Midwest. That photo was shot this past summer (June, 2017) when Dan and I took a trip to a small town car show about 50 miles from our home in Aurora, ColoRODo.

Some time ago, in anticipation of writing this book, I'd asked my nephew, Cade Sonnichsen, recently retired from the Air Force as a Lt. Colonel, to design the cover of this book since he is/was into photoshop and knew all that computer program stuff and he said he'd like to. He currently lives in San Antonio, Texas, so I'd sent him some pix I liked but he said the background was too busy/crowded and he'd have to do too much work to clean it up. He suggested we find a hill, put the sun behind us, park the car atop the hill so there would be more sky showing and shoot a bunch of pix.

We were going to Deer Trail for their car show in late June, 2017, on a two-lane highway, I spotted this small hill that I thought would be perfect and told Dan we needed to stop there on the way home and shoot some pix. I hadn't told him that I planned on using his car on the cover of this book and he was surprised when I told him that's why we were going to shoot photos that afternoon. I must have shot about two dozen different pictures and it was actually fun to try to figure out which poses would be the best for the cover…and I think we succeeded in getting the right shot for this book. FWIW, that's Dan's '54 Cadillac that he drives to shows. I usually follow in my '55 Cadillac. Dan bought this Caddy in 2002 and it took us a few years to re-do the majority of it and overhaul the engine and transmission in 2009. It's been on the road ever since.

Dan and I have always driven our cars…no matter if they were/are simple everyday vehicles or "full-on" show cars (and there are some opinions as to what a 'full on' show car is but I'll leave that up to you). I've never had a good reason to trailer a car to a summer-time show or rod run when I could simply get in, turn the key, put the car in gear and drive to the event. Yeah, there's always a chance of rain in the summer, and rain and hail in the Spring and both again late Fall, but most of the time, the rod running weather is sun shiney and great. Even in the winter –and I'm from Iowa where we REALLY had winter, I've never been afraid of driving on snow covered highways, and that never stopped my brother or I from going anywhere. We've driven our cars in just about every kind of weather from slushy roads to snow-packed mountain roads to muddy roads as you'll read in a couple of the stories in this book.

Okay, let me explain my perspective on building a "show car." When I was building my latest car- the '55 Cadillac I now own, one afternoon in the garage when I was doing something that only added to the gleam of the car, Dan accused me of building a "full-on show car." He thought I was going overboard in wanting a clean and painted chassis/engine and cleaning, painting or making things that couldn't be seen shiney…most of that stuff no one else would see while standing five feet from it. I simply told him I wasn't "building" a show car, that I was just building a really nice street car…!!! Somewhere along the way in that build, Dan accepted that I was correct in the way I wanted to build my car. It took me 5 ½ years to build my 'really nice street car" and I have never regretted doing it that way. It wins lots of awards and has been featured in several magazines. The 'next' car, my 1948 Cadillac Sedanet is being built that way as well. My cars may not be perfect in every sense of the word, or as perfect as a "pro" builder would turn it out, but there is simply no other way for me to build a car. I want a nice street car.

But, back to driving a hot rod or kustom…and don't get me wrong, there is a time and place to trailer a car. Yes, I've trailered a couple of my cars to winter indoor car shows in Albuquerque, New Mexico; Wichita, Kansas; Salt Lake City, Utah; Rapid City, South Dakota and Kansas City, Kansas…let me reiterate: IN THE WINTER. Putting a car in the trailer certainly keeps road grime off of it, and if the car were driven to an indoor winter-time show, it'd make for many more hours of cleaning, hence into the trailer it goes. No regrets.

However, the whole gist of this book is to let you know that there is absolutely no reason for you to not drive your hot rod, custom or classic. Just this past summer (2017), coming back from Good-guys event in Puyallup, Washington, we met a guy on Wyoming's Snowy Range two-lane highway. He was driving a Prius and asked about the car we were driving- Dan's 1964 Impala SS. During the conversation, he mentioned he wanted to drive his '64 Bel Air from his home in Logan, Utah, to Omaha, Nebraska where he was born but he didn't 'trust" it would make the distance. He was shocked that we had driven to Seattle in Dan's Impala and were heading home at the time. He said he thought driving an old car was only a local deal-not for long distances. Needless to say we squashed his thoughts about that right then and there! So, to those of you that feel the same, get that old car out, fill the fuel tank and take a long distance trip in it...and stay off the Interstate highways.

Dan and I have been fortunate to be able to see this great country (and Canada several times) through the windshield of several old cars...and he and I have been fortunate to be able to put up with each other over all these years. I must tell you that without Dan reading my stories and finding all the misteaks...ehrrr...uhmmmm, mistakes I've made while typing, I wouldn't look so good. In some of these stories, Dan has written a few of them and without him remembering all the places, and dates, we've been and all the highways we've driven on, these stories wouldn't be as good. He and I have been into and through 33 of the 48 contiguous states...and three times to and through (mostly western) Canada. Having said that, let me just say there's more real Americana out there on those old two-lanes than you'll ever see on a four-lane Interstate OR in the seat of an airliner at 30,000 feet! Get out there and see the USA...!!!

I started rod running, well, actually my brother, Dan, and I have been rod running since 1976...we went to our first NSRA "Nats" in 1976 in Tulsa, Oklahoma...and have looked forward to travelling this country in summers ever since then. We went to our first Good-guys event here in ColoRODo, in 1998 and in summer of 2017 to the Puyallup, Washington show and have been to several Good-guys events all across this country since then. There's a good story about the trip to Bowling Green, Kentucky and the GG's Hall of Fame Tour in 2015 in this book. We've been to Good-guys events in Puyallup and Spokane, Washington; Indianapolis, Indiana; Kansas City, Kansas; Scottsdale, Arizona; Des Moines, Iowa; and Dallas, Texas and as many NSRA events across this country. So, this book of "incidents" covers over four decades of Dan and I rod running across the United States!

Dan and I used to be the local long distance champs around here as we put on close to 15,000/20,000 miles a summer traveling cross country in our rods and kustoms, did that for about four decades and we're not done yet. However, if you drive your rod a long distance, a lot of strange things can be seen on the back roads of this country and a lot of strange things can happen on the way…worse part, you may have to stop and fix it.

As you'll see in the following stories, I hate driving Interstates and a lot of these stories happened on two-lane highways all across the United States…and in Canada. Taking a two-lane these days is akin to the pioneers in wagon-trains, blazing their own way across the prairies. While a lot of these stories fall into the "broke down" category, there are stories that are just kinda fun and some stories that are hard to believe, but true. Suffice to say, they happened while Dan and I drove our cars to and from rod runs.

Now if you haven't read any of my other books…and you should (see the back of this book for a list of my other books), and as a way of letting you know you've probably already read a lot of my writing, may I suggest many of you have been reading me since 2004! Yep, that's correct! I wrote a monthly column for Good-guys Gazette, for over 10 years…and what a great run that was…!!! Currently and for the last two years, I do feature articles for the Rod Authority website and for the Street Muscle website and I write a column for Ol' Skool Rodz magazine every other month - as of this book, I'll be starting the third year of that just after this book comes out. This book is the seventh I've done. You can find all of them on Amazon, the earlier books in the 'used' category however, but still available. The last book, Arsenal Code R.E.D. is a fictional thriller set in Denver, ColoRODo and it's available as a hardbound book or a KINDLE download.

Herein then are a few rod running stories that I call 'fix it on the side of the road.' If most of you that go rod running in your old car do some serious high mileage white line flying, you can probably relate too, I'd bet. Enjoy.

HERE WE GO...

I'll start off the following stories with a piece I wrote 20 years ago, way back in 1997 when I was editor of Kustoms of America's Magazine. With GPS these days and I-phones, Smart phones, Blue tooth, electronic tablets complete with internet and Google, I thought this story would mean something to those of us that don't use those devices to find our way across the U.S. and to those of us that keep our "hand-helds" in the glove compartment of our cars.

Dan and I had driven to several of KOA's events back east and I'd ask several people why they didn't come out west to some of our rod runs. Heard a ton of excuses why they didn't take a long trip in their cars, but the best one was "No GPS!" If you can't find your way across the U.S without a GPS, you NEED to stay home!

Over the years since, I've also found that there's a lot of car guys in my own neighborhood that won't even drive out of their city to attend a rod run - won't even drive across town to go to a local cruise! Those guys I've labeled "zip code rodders," meaning they won't even leave their own zip code to go show off their car or see some different cars...or take a long distance trip to see the USA!

So here's a nod to the past!

Roger

MAPS - A SATIRICAL LOOK

After driving back east to Pigeon Forge, Tennessee, in 1995 and the Double Date event in Richmond, Indiana, (as well as driving to Good-guys event in Indy), June, 1996, and having been to several events on the west coast...and literally ALL over this great country of ours in our cars over the course of the last twenty years, I've noticed something that's COMMON to a lot of car owners: They WON'T take a long distance trip in their cars! I've heard more excuses-"My car won't go that far!" "My car doesn't ride well!" "Take a trip in THAT? I couldn't stand to get beat up that bad for that long!" "Engine's not that good!" "Tranny's going out." "Can't get that much time off of work."

Well, I'm here to tell you that you don't have to use those excuses any more. Matter of fact, you don't need any excuse. Ya see, I've finally figured out WHY long distance trips are out of the question for so many people...something Dan and I have known for YEARS! Something the folks at NHRA(National Hot Rod Association) and NSRA (National Street Rod Association) have known for over twenty-five years now...something that the guys at Good-guys have known for a long time and something only recently discovered by the guys at Petersen Publishing (in California) and something the guys at Super Chevy magazine have known for over 10 years now...THE BIG SECRET is out of the bag and here it is...MAPS...yeah, ROAD MAPS! Did you know that EVERY state has its own map? It's true! Did you know that every ROAD in that state is on that map? Yeah, seriously! EVERY road, even dirt roads! Here's something else I'll bet you didn't know...if you take EACH state map and stick them together, you'll find that the roads CONTINUE into the next state! Yeah, that is even true! Dan and I have done it lots over the past twenty years and we're still doing it!

Here's something else I'll bet you didn't know...YOUR state isn't at the end of the world! You won't fall into some deep dark chasm that you can't get back out of when you get to the state line at the end of your map! The roads actually CONNECT and lo and behold, you can continue right into and through that next state, too! One thing you will have to do is stop and pick up a map of that state. Most gas stations have them, and we've found that most are FREE if you buy their gas. If you put four or five maps together, you'll notice that you can get farther and farther from home, and closer and closer to the EVENT of your choice! Not to worry, simply reverse the procedure, and your direction, and you can follow the roads on the map and that'll take you on roads going right back home! You'll find, believe it or not...all of the Interstate Highways are finished and all are four-lanes! Have been for over forty years now and most are in pretty good shape.

Dan and I don't run the Interstates that much, we prefer the two-lanes, but if our '57, with only four inches of ground clearance, can maneuver the Interstates in this country, your car can too! Here's something else you MIGHT not know ...all along these roads there are buildings called MOTELS. I'm guessing here but I think that word came from two: MOtorists and hoTEL...and you can, for a small fee, spend the night there. Most have beds and a TV, so it's almost like being at home, even a bathroom is included in the price. If you ask nicely, the person behind the desk taking your "rent" money will give you a wake-up call in the morning (yes, there are also phones in each room in case you want to check on the cat while you're gone!), all you have to do state the time you want to be awakened. The best part about a motel is that most times you can PARK your car directly in front of the door of the room you're staying in. Sometimes you'll find motels that have second floors or third and higher...avoid those. Although they have balconies, you'll find it's difficult to put on your pants and try to run down the stairs each time you hear strange noises in the night coming from outside your room! Don't worry too much about those noises...you will hear lots of strange noises in a motel room. Most don't have anything to do with your car parked outside. Simply leave the drapes open a crack so you can get up and look out.

Back to those maps...when you get yours, have someone take charge of it. That person can be called the NAVIGATOR. That person can decide what roads you should take. Listen to them closely, they will tell you where you are going and what roads/highway you should take.

   Now if more than one car goes with you, you get to be the TOUR LEADER since you have a navigator that understands how to read maps. Or you can designate someone else to be the leader. That's what R & C does with their Americruise. They designate people in different parts of the country as Tour Leaders. Those people are in charge of the MAPS...NOTICE that word is plural... they get maps from each state they are going through so the route can be planned ahead of time. This is a good thing because sometimes the map(s), having laid on the navigator's lap all day, can become soiled with coffee, soft drinks, Twinkies, chocolate, Secret Sauce and a variety of other foodstuffs. When that happens, the map becomes hard to read and you can get lost. That's something you are not wont to do. Sometimes, however, that can be fun! Anyway, that's one of the reasons R & C started the Americruise...so they could show lots of people that they discovered MAPS! I don't know who originally showed them maps, but they are certainly letting lots of other people know and that's why I'm sharing this. Now you have no excuse not to come out west...or go anywhere else for that matter. But don't believe me, go to a gas station and get your own map...if you want to see more roads than just those in your state, simply go to WalMart, or your nearest State Farm Insurance Agent...they have large books, called an Atlas, that has all the states bound together, in alphabetical order and in COLOR! These show major roads, but for two lane excursions, you should really get and use a ROAD MAP!

   It's a lot more fun than staying at home and there's some great scenery out there. See YOU at an event, OUT OF YOUR STATE, next summer?

THE MINNESOTA INCIDENT

This incident occurred in my home town of Denison, Iowa, on our way to Minnesota and after driving 650 miles from our home in Denver, ColoRODo.

July 1977. Denison, Iowa. We'll start this story off with a bit of back story: we were off to St. Paul, Minnesota for the Street Machine Nats and we'd planned to spend the night with my Mother, still living in southwestern Iowa...650 miles from Denver. I'd informed her a few days before we left there would be nine of us making the trip. She made reservations at the local motel for our traveling buddies – Phil Roth and Dave Hudson in Phil's '57 Chevy two-door, Doug Boettcher and Tim Graham in Doug's '66 Impala hardtop, Tom Stover, his wife and daughter in their '56 Chevy and my bro, Dan, and I were in my '57 Chevy two door.

After a wild, fun filled, not-the-speed-limit, lane-swapping, race-me 10-hour trip on Interstate 80, we arrived at Mom's house at 9:30 PM. It was agreed we'd leave in the morning, make St. Paul by late afternoon, in time for the local cruise at Porky's. After saying our hellos and having a snack, I volunteered to lead the group to the motel. I backed my '57, (at that time, pearl white with brown flames-yeah I know, the flames weren't very "trad", but I was learning and in my attempt at being "different" I laid them out. If you intend to be different, make sure it works...!!!) out of the driveway, turned the steering wheel, heard a 'pop'... and dismissed it. Ran over something...no worries. I straightened the wheel, gunned the engine and shot down the street -- showing off. Something didn't feel quite right. I slowed to make a right turn at the next intersection. The Chevy started to drift toward the curb, I tried to correct, it stayed its course. I braked. The right tire bounced against the curb and I stopped, hard. Turned the wheel to the left, felt "loose," attempted backing up. Turned left and right. The car won't follow my directions, nothing seems to work, not steering correctly. Give the steering wheel a spin -

- it made five complete revolutions before it slowed. Uh-oh, steering wheel no longer connected to steering box. I didn't know it at the second I backed out of the driveway, but the 'pop' was the steering shaft nearly shearing off inside the box. I started to shake...realizing just how lucky I'd been... I'd just driven 650 miles at 75-80 mph, with bursts of speed up to 100-110 mph as all of us played on the way. Why did the shaft break conveniently in Mom's driveway? We were still alive...was it luck it didn't break...or was someone riding with Dan and I ? Watching over us? I'm certain that was the first time my guardian angel rode with Dan and I.

Now what? Fix the car, right? I maintain that IF you can't fix your car on the side of the road, you'd best stay home (or trailer it). In the morning, after we got the car back in Mom's driveway, it took most of the day to find another '57 Chevy steering box. We called the two junk yards around town and then called several more in nearby smaller towns. No luck. A friend that I went to HS with had stopped by to see us and scoped out our problem...said his brother still had a '57 4-door on the farm but there wasn't much left on it. We kinda figured the steering box wouldn't be gone...they usually don't "break"...and it was there. First we had to find the car...it was 'buried' in weeds about six feet tall and we couldn't even see it...it hadn't been moved in years and in Iowa, weeds grow fast.

Donnie, my friend, hooked up the car to his tractor via a chain and pulled it to the barn, every snake, mouse, spider and wasp abandoned the car quickly. He then raised it up so we could unbolt the box and column. We had to remove the whole box and column from the bottom of the car since Chevy didn't put in a rag joint in 1957. Once out and back home, we had to raise my '57 high enough to do the reverse of taking it out...problem: didn't have much around the house to hold it up, we found cut up tree trunks, stacked them under the frame to get it high enough to feed the column back up through the mast and bolt the box to the frame, slide on the pitman arm, bolt the steering wheel back on and hook the electrical together.

When we were done, I was covered in sweat and filth and it was late afternoon. After I took a shower, I took the car for a test drive to see if it was all working correctly. With it pronounced good for the long haul, we decided to leave the next morning.

That night during dinner and anticipating the rest of the trip, the conversation got around to 'what if'? Postulations made, questions pondered and blessings counted made us feel relatively good. At dessert, Mom reiterated her stand on my driving, ever since I was 16 and got my license - I remembered her years - old warning, her nagging feeling that I would be killed in an automobile accident and "This could be the start of it. Please be careful on the rest of the trip, son."

But, that isn't the end of this "incident"...things were going smooth until we got to Albert Lea, Minnesota...Tom Stover said he had some grinding noises coming from the rear of his car...we pulled into town and found an empty lot...deduced it was a rear wheel bearing...now where are we going to get a rear wheel bearing for a '56 Chevy...and get it installed...???

The parts store said "we can order one for you, take a day or two."

"No, we don't have that kind of time, any junkyards close?"

Just on the outskirts of town was an old yard...and "Yep, think I got a '56 way in the back, don't know what's left of it though."

Both rear axles were still in the housing...our pal Dave "Wooley" Hudson was a brute of a guy...he took a Chevy rim, reversed it, bolted it loosely to the axle...and jerked. It took two jerks to release the axle from the housing. The bearing felt good so back to Tom's '56...using a very unsafe bumper jack, we raised the car high enough to remove the wheel and tire and proceeded to do the same thing we did on the other '56...did I mention the afternoon was really hot...so hot that the asphalt around Tom's '56 was very soft. Bet I know what you're thinking and you'd be correct...the bumper jack was beginning to lean. It was sinking into the asphalt...two of us held that car from tipping over until the axle was back in, the wheel/tire back on. We cleaned up in McDonalds' and cooled off in their A/C, ate a late lunch and headed on to St. Paul. Tom never had a bit of trouble after that and neither did I. Our pal, Doug and his 409" powered '66 Impala and Phil in his '57,were the only cars that didn't have problems. A little aside about that trip, back then we all ran CB's, always had a great time talking back and forth...somewhere on I-80, a trucker, going the other direction, asked where we were going and why we had a "late model" in between the '57's and the '56...I told the driver that we might need spare parts on a trip like this. Remember that Doug, Tim? Our "spare parts car" didn't do us a bit of good though.

Relaxing at home on my patio in the summer evenings as the sun dips below Denver's purple mountains, I think about Dad's occupation: truck driver, and figure that's where I got my love of driving. Dad used to travel the highways of this great country weekly in his eighteen-wheeler...and loved it. Even when our family went on vacation, we didn't fly. We drove, everywhere we went, and we drove all over this country seeing the sights. Dad was the consummate sight-seeing tourist. At times like this I think of Mom's "warning" and, well, this incident happened late seventies, one great big bunch of years ago, and I'm still driving all over the country in the summers (Dan and I used to be the "travel kings" around Denver, except, we were never home...we'd log 15,000 to 20,000 miles a summer rod running)...suffice to say, my guardian angel rides with me (and my brother, Dan) all the time as you'll read in the next stories...

Two years after that incident, we went back to St. Paul in our street rods, this time for the Street Rod Nats. I'd found a raggedy old 1940 Studebaker coop at a local swap meet in August, 1977, and decided to build a street rod...in time, the old Studey got painted, upholstered, a new engine, new wheels and tires installed and my indoctrination into rodding was initiated and a ton of miles happened in that car and my brother's street rod.

Read on, there's more incidents in our rod running travels across the US - perfect examples of fixing stuff on the side of the road and a few other stories about different 'incidents' other than breaking things. When we first started rod running we had no idea how a long distance trip would play out...at the time, our vehicles were very street-worthy - around town...!!! We found that not to be the case on a long distance trip and things were subject to breaking.

THE CALIFORNIA INCIDENT

This was the first time we ventured to California in a street rod. This incident occurred on the way to Merced, California, for one of Gary Meadors' NSRA events.

August, 1978. California Highway One. So, there we were, cruising along a four-lane highway somewhere in California, after a two day trip from our home in ColoRODo - Dan and I are in my unfinished '40 Stude rod and pal, Phil Roth and his GF in his black '46 Ford coop (he'd traded a derelict '29 roadster for it - straight across)...I'd just gotten my '40 Studey on the road...and by on the road, I mean drivable and licensed...not finished by any means -- the seats were covered in an old tan blanket held together with safety pins, duct tape and snaps, the door panels were non-existent, the dash was still red-colored original woodgrain with brown streaks down the front of it where the water had leaked in from the hard windshield rubber, all the glass was still original with gray bubbles between the laminations in the corners and our feet rested on a bare metal floor with no carpet, or heat killer, of any kind.

When the car became roadworthy earlier that spring, we'd decided on a trip to Merced, California, for one of the last NSRA events in August of 1978...Gary Meadors was their director at the time, some time before he started Good-guys, and we had decided to make a two week vacation of it – sight-seeing, taking our time, having fun in our 'new' hot rods.

My old Studey was fitted with a stock 400" SBC, a T400 tranny, a tilt column with column shifter, headers, Corvette style side exhaust in place of the running boards and heated coils up front to get the correct street rod nose down attitude. It ran old 14" 5-spoke mags and I'd primered it in two tones of hot rod gray (light on the body, dark on the fenders) and I'd laid out some copper colored flames on the hood and fenders...I "outlined" them with a Buegler striper in a couple of colors and the white lettered rear tires were so wide they almost stuck outside the fenders...it was close, but they were just under the edge of the fender... keep in mind this was 1978...only 8 years after the first Nats and I was all of 35 years old.

It wasn't too bad when we first started out from home...up over the mountains out of Denver on I-70 in cool weather...running along about 60 mph since the speed limit was only 55...but once we got into Utah...it got hot...not only from the actual August weather, but the heat coming off the firewall and floor of the Stude was enough to make us not want to go any farther. But we'd planned on this for several months and we weren't going to let a little heat get to us. Because of the heat, and neither of our cars were equipped with A/C (hard to find in 1978), we decided to cross the salt flats at night so we holed up in a couple of motel rooms in western Salt Lake City late afternoon, caught some sleep, until about midnight.

At that time of the night, there was literally no traffic on I-80 and the breeze coming in the windows was cool...especially at about 90 mph...no sense wasting time by running only 60 or 70 mph. Phil decided to see what his Ford would do (running a simple 283" SBC in it) so he pulled alongside me and pointed...meaning 'let's go.' We did...for several miles we went as young and dumb, with new unproven cars, 'racing' across the flats with all the abandon of two indestructible youngsters.

The 'race' ended when a bright green light flashed across the sky in front of us...it was fluorescent colored and moving rapidly across both our windshields...and being extremely dark out on the flats, it was almost like daylight when the meteor happened across the sky and lit everything around us. It scared me at first until I realized what it was...but that was enough to slow us for the rest of the night.

We decided to go to Reno and then up around Tahoe and down the long hill on Highway 50 over to Merced for the event ...once there, we had a good time for the weekend but my ol' Stude sure was frowned on...I think the whole problem was it wasn't a '32 Ford, wasn't painted and at that time, it wasn't looked upon as a street rod...it didn't matter a lot to me cuz it was MY hot rod and I'd driven my very first hot rod a long distance...just to prove to myself that I could build a "long distance driver." From Merced, we drove over to

San Francisco and dropped off a Denver buddy so he could catch a flight home...we did some sight-seeing in the big city and found Highway One near Pacifica...we were going to Disneyland...!!!

Highway One is a great scenic highway...but we didn't get to see too much...it was cloudy, rainy and wet the whole way down the coast....occasionally we'd get out of the low lying clouds but it didn't last long...and when we got closer to LA, the smog began to be overwhelming.

Somewhere around Santa Barbara, we were enjoying what scenery we could see and running along at about 75 or so, but cars were passing us by like we were standing still...Phil decided if Porsches and Mercedes could run at 85 and 90, his street rod could, too. We ran CB's at that time and Phil figured we could keep up, so he yelled at me and we both kicked it up...that is, until all of a sudden, all those cars slowed to 55...neither Phil or I could figure out why. So we just went flying around them to the head of the pack. It didn't take long until we found out why...the red and blue flashes of the CHP glared in our rear view mirrors.

I was the first to be pulled over. The CHP officer came to my window and asked me for my license. "Do you know how fast you were going...???"

"According to my speedometer, I was running right at 60 mph."

He didn't say much after that except to tell me to follow him until he "could get the other guy stopped." As the Porsches and Mercedes' went around me and the CHP officer, there were smiles, cat-calls and gestures. It didn't take long for me and the CHP to find Phil cuz he was paying attention, saw me get pulled over since I was running behind him. He'd pulled off the side of the road to wait for me...once all three of us were on the side of the road, I got out of my car and approached Phil. The officer stopped me in my tracks and said, "Don't you say one word til I talk to your pal."

"Yessir."

"Your license please, sir," he said to Phil.

After Phil handed him his license and he looked at it, he then asked Phil how fast he was going.

"Sir, my speedometer read exactly 60 mph," Phil said. "Is there a problem?"

The CHP shook his head, handed us back our licenses and said, "Since you're both from out of state, I'm letting you two off with a warning. But let me make this warning a bit more specific...I clocked both of you at 75, I suggest you get those ancient speedometers checked...and for your own safety, and to avoid a speeding ticket, hold it to 40 on your speedometer, that'll put you right about 55."

Neither Phil nor I knew what the other was going to say to the CHP Officer, and neither one of us had told the other what to say in case we got pulled over...we just got lucky.

We drove on into Anaheim and Disneyland...and had a great time.

THE MEMPHIS INCIDENT

This incident occurred while Dan and I drove to Memphis for the NSRA (National Street Rod Association) Nats. This was only the second time we'd gone to a major rod run anywhere.

July, 1980. Mulberry, Arkansas. We were headed to Memphis, Tennessee, for the Nats and my Studey was looking good in its shiny new Cadillac LimeFire Mist paint. The interior lacked finishing but we figured with the new engine/tranny we'd be okay…we were, for a while.

When I put the Stude on the road, with a used engine, in 1978…it burned a bit too much oil in the two years I drove it. So in April, 1980, overhaul time -- in a one car garage, attached to my condo. My Stude barely fit, had to pull the front clip and store it overhead (read that- wired up to the garage ceiling) in order to pull engine/trans. Once the 400" engine was out, it went to my engine building friend…he was the type to do it correctly, not cut corners. It took a month before I got the engine back, the tranny was redone, too.

Once back together, I put about 500 miles on it around town…with a few 60-80 mile trips to nearby towns to break it in…the engine felt good, strong and ran great…and it didn't burn oil…!!! While pulling the engine, my bro, Dan and I talked about a long distance trip again…so we discussed Memphis – had never been there.

My friend Mike Heeren had been building a '48 Chevy coupe but a SBC wasn't good enough for him… he opted for a 455" Buick …it was a tight fit, but Mike got it all figured out in time and mentioned he and his wife wanted to go with Dan and I…then a day or two later, my son (eight at the time) and daughter (14 at the time) asked if they could go….how could I say no? "Uhm, Dan, four of us in my old coop is going to be too tight…can you drive your own car?" Well, Dan's '47 Chevy wasn't ready to go…so he had to drive his '73 Dodge Dart. We left home Monday …one hundred and sixty miles later, the engine in my Stude started missing. "Oh great...my new engine is dying already...!!!" It felt like a plug had fouled or a wire had fallen off...I killed the engine and coasted to the side. We were just outside of Burlington, ColoRODo, with the hood open. All the plug wires were on...but when I started the car my bro said the noise sounded like it was coming from the valve cover. I pulled the cover -- found one rocker arm split right down the middle...the nut and rocker ball still attached to the stud...I pulled the pushrod to see if it was bent but it was okay.

My bro drove me into Burlington, home of the Hitchcock Brothers...street rod builders extraordinaire because I was aware they had SBC's laying around. There was one in back and we pulled two rocker arms -- needed one...got an "extra one - just in case." Hoped it wasn't needed. By the time we got back to the car, the engine had cooled enough to fix it. Fifteen minutes later we were moving. Our first over-night stop was to be Kansas City...didn't make it...forty miles out of KC, another rocker broke...I heard this one coming...it started ticking and got louder. By the time I shut the engine off, it had split...same as the first. Luckily, I had that spare. That night, at the motel, I pulled both valve covers, checked to see if they were adjusted too tightly. No problem there.

In the morning, Joplin, Missouri, was our destination, visit relatives...didn't have a problem all day and on Wednesday morn, we again hit the highway. In case you hadn't noticed, we like to take scenic routes...south through the Ozark "Mountains," planning to get to Ft. Smith by nightfall. Two-lanes have a way of slowing you down so you can smell the roses...especially following RV's going up the hills, but if I recall it wasn't roses I smelled, more like diesel exhaust. We couldn't find a vacant motel in Ft. Smith but we did in Alma, a few miles down the road.

Up the next morning, I figured we'd get into Memphis about 3 PM...looked forward to it...but my engine had other ideas. No more than ten miles out of town, I got the ticking noise again...this was getting ridiculous...I needed to have a talk with my engine builder! We slipped off the interstate at Mulberry, Arkansas, nothing more than a blink-of-the-eye town...now where are we going to find rocker arms in this burg? No parts stores, not much except a gas station on the corner. We asked if there were any junk yards around, were told outside of town, back west on a couple of miles of dirt road...ehhhr, dirt path--tall trees lined both sides and weeds grew in the center. No, I didn't hear any "Deliverance" music cuz my Studey was making plenty of noise as I was coaxing it past the yard gate. I was expecting someone holding a shotgun demanding to know what we wanted...all three of us pulled in next to a dilapidated building and the owner, wearing baggy overalls and a pinstriped railman's hat greeted us. "What can I do for you gents? Them are some pretty fancy cars you got." I explained about the cars, where we were headed, and were from, making small talk and finally got around to explaining my problem.

"Oh sure, got me a couple of buckets full of 'em out by the barn, don't know where though, but I'll be glad to take ya out there, we can look." We followed, between the old house and another building on a narrow path -- all kinds of metal piled up, plenty of old stoves, refrigerators and other appliances stacked, past a couple of salvageable fifties Fords and wooden file cabinets stacked as high as the roof. I was afraid they'd fall...and I could just see the headlines: "ColoRODo folk in strange old cars buried alive by wooden filing cabinets!" They'd never find us anyway! I hurried past, figuring he'd have at least one old Chevy out there somewhere.

As we walked, for some unknown reason, he told us about his 6 foot pet Bull snake that usually lounges around at the barn we were headed for...especially after he'd eaten. Dan stopped in his tracks. "Uhm, I'll wait by my car. You go on."

Sure enough, there by the barn all kinds of engines were piled up. Cool...and a couple of buckets of rocker arms and pushrods "Pick some out," the old guy pointed. "I'm gonna check on Jethro, the snake. Don't see him anywhere, he might be lying in wait for a snack. Be right back." Mike and I pulled six clean ones out of one bucket by the time he got back. "How much?"

"Couple bucks," he said. Back at the car, I pulled the passenger side valve cover and replaced two – one already broken and another just barely together. With the car running smooth, we found our way out to the highway.

That afternoon we got into Memphis and found our motel downtown...it was hot and humid, ugh. It was so hot the newly laid asphalt on the fair-grounds actually stuck to the soles of our shoes and tire tracks were sunk into it all over the grounds. We went swimming in the rooftop pool every night since the temperature never dipped below 98, even after midnight, the humidity was just as high. During the three days we were there, we visited Sun Studios (where the "Million dollar quartet" of Carl Perkins, Johnny Cash, Jerry Lee Lewis and Elvis recorded) and took a trip out to Graceland...we could actually walk right up to the house and the garden where his grave was. There were no fences or admission to get into the place at the time and we parked on the street next to the house.

After the Sunday awards, we lit out for St. Louis...outside of Cape Girardeau, another rocker arm broke, I replaced it and we spent the night in St. Louis. I checked the rest to see if there were any that were about to break, all looked fine. Halfway across Missouri, near Columbia, another broke -- this time the rocker ball had busted a hole in the arm but it didn't snap in half, I found all the pieces laying just under the stud –luckily, none fell into the oil galley. At the rate those broke, I decided to take the three spares and replace those that looked like they were going to break. In total, I'd replaced eight on one head and two on the other...since I didn't have any "spares" left, I hoped we'd get home without breaking more. Fortunately, we did...next day, I found one more cracked and replaced it. I still, to this day, do not know why those rocker arms broke and no one has been able to explain to me why...and, strangest thing, I've never had any break since...and the old Studey logged 140,000 miles on that same engine...other than breaking rocker arms, it's been a good one...and it just goes to show ya them old SBC's are plentiful – anywhere...!!! Maybe that's why they are so popular.

Authors note: – I used to carry a coffee can full of rocker arms and pushrods in the trunk in my old Studey but I sold that car in 2012. It was sold to a guy in the Netherlands – yep, across the ocean. It was then sold to a guy in Germany and he, in turn, sold the car to someone in Austria. One day on Facebook, I saw a picture of the Stude at a show in Austria and the car hadn't changed a bit from the time I sold it. That was the last I'd heard or seen the old Studey and that was in 2016.

THE LAS VEGAS INCIDENT

An old car for sale, beautiful scenery, a muddy show grounds and a major car problem! This incident occurred while Dan and I took a 10 day rod running vacation.

July, 1983. Las Vegas, Nevada. We'd planned a trip to the Street Rod Nats in Oklahoma City, we'd never been to that event. The plan was to spend the weekend there then on Monday head over to Las Vegas the following weekend for the Super Run. I was driving my '40 Studebaker coop and Dan was driving his '47 Chevy Aerosedan. Rhonda and Bill Gordon had decided to go with us in their '36 Chevy sedan so we had a nice three car caravan. We left Denver at 6 AM, took I-70 to Limon and then caught Highway 287, a decent two-lane going straight south. Lamar would be our first stop for fuel. Campo was next, just before the Oklahoma border. As we motored through that Campo, Dan spotted a '48 Chevy two door sedan sitting next to an old garage/gas station. We pulled in and asked about the car, the owner said "Yeah, it's for sale. You interested?" Of course we were, IF he didn't want a million dollars for it like most people did. I think he was asking $250.00 for it. It didn't run so we knew we'd have to trailer it home at a later date. Dan said OK and gave him a $50.00 deposit and said we'd come back in a few weeks to pick it up. We figured it'd be a good project for later on but unfortunately, it never got built and Dan ended up selling it to a friend a couple of years later. Back on the road, we finally got to Oklahoma City late afternoon and found our motel. The next day the Nats started and we enjoyed the weekend, the fair-grounds and the burnouts on Meridian Street a couple of those nights. We got to see a lot of new cars we'd never see at home. On Monday, Dan and I headed west on I-40, Bill and Rhonda headed back to Denver. Along the way we found parts of old Route 66 and drove some of that. There were lots of old sights along that old highway and the road took us right to our over-night stay in Albuquerque.

Tuesday morning we did some sightseeing around the city and took a chair lift ride up Sandia Peak to see the valley below. Later that afternoon we arrived in Flagstaff but our motel reservation was in Sedona, south of Flagstaff. We arrived late that night and had no idea what kind of scenery we'd missed on the way down. The next morning was a shocker when we stepped out onto the balcony of the motel room *(see the next story: "The Sedona Incident").*

After our over-night stay in Sedona, we drove the 27 miles back up to and through Flagstaff and on to the south rim of the Grand Canyon. After spending a few hours there we drove to Williams, Arizona, and stayed over-night there. Since we had a few days to kill and we weren't that far from Lake Havasu, we decided to go see the London Bridge in the morning, but talk about hot when we got there! With no A/C in either car, coming down off the high plateau into the desert was like stepping into a blast furnace...we found the London Bridge, checked it out and drove around Havasu before we decided it was way too hot around there and headed north for Kingman. Once past Kingman, only a few more miles and we'd be able to drive over the Hoover Dam... first time we'd been there and the lake was capacity...water was shooting out of the spillway full force. As we were climbing out of the canyon the dam was built in, Dan radioed that the rear-end in his '47 was starting to howl...wasn't sounding well so we'd better figure out what was going bad. It didn't take us long to get from the dam to downtown Las Vegas.

Our room reservations were at the Tropicana hotel, of course, that's where the Super Run was to be held, on their expansive golf course. We registered for the show, unloaded the trunks of luggage and proceeded to check out Dan's car. After we jacked it up and ran it in gear, we figured one of the rear wheel bearings was the problem. OK, now where are we going to find a rear wheel bearing for a '57 Chev rear-end in Vegas? Maybe an auto parts store might have one. Yep, first one we phoned had the bearing but no, they couldn't remove the old one or press a new one on! They suggested a nearby machine shop and gave us directions to it so we jumped in my Studey and set off to find the parts store somewhere in North Las Vegas. Since it was after six by the time we got to the parts store, we figured the repair would have to wait til the morning. The store guys said the machine shop closed at noon on Saturdays. We found the store, purchased the bearing and rented their axle puller. In the morning, we jacked up the car in the Tropicana parking lot and pulled the axles-passenger's side was good so it had to be driver's side. Off to the machine shop to have the old one removed and new one pressed on…on the way back we returned the axle puller, got the deposit back and put the axle back in Dan's '47. Late Saturday morning we drove both cars to the golf course and enjoyed seeing lots of new hot rods and kustom cars parked on the green grass.

We enjoyed the show and of course, enjoyed the Las Vegas Casinos at night. Monday morning we headed for Los Angeles and to Long Beach to see Howard Hughes's airplane - the Spruce Goose and go next door to the Queen Mary. From there we drove north to the Sequoia National Park to see the giant trees, then drove to Yosemite National Park. From there it was on to Reno, Nevada. We took I-80 to the Bonneville salt flats, through Salt Lake City and up through Wyoming and back home from there. In 17 days, we'd traveled through 9 states and put on 4,878 miles on both cars with only the one minor problem. Moral of the story: If you can't fix your car on the side of the road, stay home. And that is something Dan or I have never done..!!!

THE SEDONA INCIDENT

On the way to Las Vegas, this incident caught us off guard. This is a continuation of the previous story, about how we ended up in Sedona, Arizona.

July, 1983. Mid-U.S. So, there we were, halfway between Oklahoma City and Las Vegas, running along at about 65 per...from our Denver home, we'd gone to Oklahoma City, OK, for the 1983 NSRA Nats...and were headed to Las Vegas, NV, for the "First Annual Super Run '83," taking a couple of weeks to do some sight-seeing as well. An aside to that, I think the "Super Run" lasted only two years and then died a quiet death. And that's OK cuz we never made it past the First Annual anyway...much because the First Annual was almost a bust...the event was sponsored by a casino on their own golf course, of all things, and I'd say they didn't much know how to put on a rod run...!!! At any rate, we were driving our street rods at the time cuz that's the only thing we had...the rad '57 had not been found on the used car lot, and not built yet... and the gray car ('57 two door) was still in Iowa, supposedly getting redone...but that's a story for another time...and Dan's '64 Impala SS had not been purchased yet either. Matter of fact, both of our street rods were fairly new at the time...mine having gotten roadworthy in 1978 and Dan's '47 Chevy Aerosedan roadworthy in 1980...but both finished in time to go to Oklahoma City a couple of years later in typical street rod style - new paint, new interior, tilt columns, CB's and great music systems to keep us awake on long trips like this. My son, Chris, at the time 12 years old, was riding with me on this trip...Dan was by himself...and remember, this was a time of cheap gasoline and even cheaper motel rooms, rod running/vacationing was fun.

We stayed over-night in Albuquerque, NM, at some motel we liked (the details of which are unimportant). In the morning we called the motel's 1 800 number to get a reservation for Flagstaff, Arizona, our next stopover, figured it'd be easier than 'hoping' we could find one when we got there. We were told that the motel in Flagstaff was booked but there was a room available in Sedona.

"OK, how far is that from Flagstaff?" I asked the reservationist, having never heard of Sedona, Arizona.

"Twenty-seven miles south of Flagstaff," the agent said.

Well, that was twenty-seven miles out of our way…but we knew there wasn't much past Flagstaff where we could stay anyway, Kingman being the next 'largest' town before heading up to Vegas, and in 1983, Kingman was little more than a gas stop –not much there. "That's not bad, we can do that easily enough. Book us in there." I replied.

With the motel taken care of for the night, all we had to do was get there. As normal for our rod running trips, playing tourist was a priority… we'd take an exit off the Interstate for some attraction…The Painted Desert was one, The Petrified Forest National Park was another, some times we'd take a thirty, fifty or 75 mile 'detour' to see something we'd hadn't known about…Dan was great with his maps…he could find the really obscure little out of the way attractions. Once through the attraction, we'd climb back onto the Interstate and head for our ultimate destination.

Daylight was beginning to fade as we neared Flagstaff and it was clouding up…looked like it was going to rain…not a problem, Sedona isn't that much farther. Once off the Interstate, the road signs told us Sedona was only 25 miles south on a two-lane.

"Piece of cake," Dan said over the CB, "twenty-five minutes and we're there."

I was leading in the '40 Stude, running along at 60-65 mph, Dan followed a few car lengths behind in his '47 Chevy. The highway was good, tall pines lined both sides of the road, what was left of the setting sunlight filtered through the trees, casting the whole highway in endless pointed shadows. It was a nice drive and the gently falling rain glistened on the windshield…a bit harder to see but we're not 'racing' to Sedona. Soon it was dark enough to turn on the headlights…I no more than do that than a yellow 'sharp right turn' warning sign flashed by…whoa, wait…straight ahead, the highway is gone-nothing but tall pines ahead of me! The highway is off to my immediate right and I slam into that hard right curve in a second…oh-oh, too fast, too fast…glom on the brakes as I go into the corner hard, cranking on the steering wheel, tires protesting. I yell at my son to grab the CB mic and tell Dan to back it down as the corner is way too sharp. My heart in my throat as we make it around the corner safely and head down the hill at a somewhat slower clip, I glanced off to the left of me, a good distance below me I see lights shining in the darkness…what are we getting into…??? The road sign warns of a sharp left ahead, I slow even more…don't want to repeat that last corner. As we go down the mountain side it got a lot darker, the sun effectively hidden behind the mountain tops.

"That was a sharp corner," Dan said through the CB. "I didn't even see the warning sign."

"I did! Good thing I was paying at least a bit of attention to the road," I said. "Looks like we're in for a down hill run for a while, I see headlights coming up from a ways below."

We switched back and forth on the road for quite a while…it's now too dark to see anything except the lines on the highway and headlight coming at us. We were apparently going down into some sort of canyon and we hadn't yet reached the bottom, we'd been driving for quite a while. Dan told me via CB that we've been heading down for over 30 minutes now…and of course, at only 20-25 mph, it would take some time to cover any distance.

Finally we started to see a few houses alongside the road…and a creek running parallel to the road, we crossed over it once or twice…in the distance we can occasionally glance more lights through the trees…must be getting close to Sedona.

The road leveled out, the tall trees end and in a quick second there is the town…Sedona. We find our motel without any problem, pull into the lot and check in. A restaurant is close so we grab a bite…the conversation goes back to the very sharp corner at the top of the canyon and our guardian angels watching over us; the hour drive it took to get to the bottom of the canyon ("only 27 miles south." I recall the operator saying) and where exactly we are…the map we brought in was no help. Guess we'll get a chance to see what we missed in the morning as we head back up to Flagstaff and then on into Vegas.

The morning brings bright sunshine coming in through the draped windows…I'd noticed last night there was a small patio off the room so I pulled the drapes open, slid the door sideways and stepped onto the patio…POW! WOW! Hit me right in the face…what a view…!!! Didn't expect this!

"Dan, get your butt out of bed and check this out," I yelled back into the room.

The sheer gold/red canyon walls were almost right on top of us, could reach out and touch them it seemed, several hundred feet tall and straight up and down. We had no idea what we'd driven into last night because of the darkness.

After breakfast and viewing the magnificent spires and rock walls surrounding the town as we drove around checking it out, we headed back up what we found out was called "Oak Creek Canyon." It took us several hours to get to the top of the canyon as we had to stop numerous times to check out the kids playing in creek, sliding down the slick rock into pools and shooting pictures of our cars in every scenic spot we could find.

Our final stop was at the corner we'd almost missed…the overlook showed us it was a good thing we made the corner as there was nothing but thin air past the four foot rock wall "railing"…talk about dodging a bullet again. We were beginning to trust our guardian angels. What a view it was, too.

Our little 'side trip' to our 'reserved' motel turned into quite an adventure, another incident in our rod running travels…and we learned one more time that there is more to see in this country, tucked into parts of the country you'd never expect to be beautiful. If you've never been to Sedona, take a trip there, it's gorgeous.

THE HEADLIGHT INCIDENT

This incident occurred while Dan and I took a three-week vacation. We went east to go west! Confused? Read on and you'll understand.

July, 1984. Mid-Nebraska. When we first started rod running back in 1977, we had no idea how a long distance trip would play out...at the time, our vehicles were very street-worthy, around town...!!! We found out many times, after a few miles of steady driving on the highway, things were subject to breaking. A little back story on this incident first - in April of 1984, I'd found a radical chopped '57 Chevy Bel Air hardtop on a used car lot in Englewood, ColoRODo...it was just about junk but I could see some potential...and after finding out it was a '57 Chevy (I actually couldn't tell what it was and I'm a '57 Chevy aficionado), I could really see the potential...I had to have it. I called my brother, Dan, and told him to come down and look at the car with me...needless to say, we went in on it together and purchased it.

Without going into a lot of detail here, suffice to say it took my brother and I from April to July to take care of the boatload of mechanical problems and electrical problems to get the car roadworthy...our ultimate goal was to drive it to Des Moines, Iowa, for the KKOA Lead Sled Spectacular at the end of July...and meet our friends Ed & Judy Banes there...they would go early to the visit relatives in Council Bluffs, Iowa, and then on to Des Moines...we'd meet them there.

Around the third weekend in July, we thought we finally had the car ready to show off at the Lead Sleds...a week previous to that, we finally decided on trailering the car cuz we weren't 100% sure the old survivor really was roadworthy so the plan was to leave on Thursday night after work for the 10 hour trip. We managed to get the car loaded Wednesday evening on an open trailer. Thursday evening everything seemed fine until we got on the Interstate and kicked up the speed...suffice to say, we didn't even get up to speed...!!! Big problem...the '72 Scout Dan had simply wouldn't pull a car on a 20 foot trailer...well, hold on, it did pull it, but any speed over 45 mph and the trailer started swaying...bad. ... Dan's short wheelbase Scout just wouldn't keep the trailer from weaving back and forth... and neither of us was about to drive like that for 650 miles. So, back home, what to do now...???

Unload the '57, unload the Scout...load our stuff in the '57 and both of us jump in...guess we're going to have to drive the '57 if we're going and hope the Chevy is roadworthy.

It took about 200 miles before I quit listening to all the strange sounds the Chevy was making...we'd never had the car out on the highway since everything we did had been relatively time consuming...matter of fact, we'd only done a few around-our-area miles...nothing very far away anyway. The old 283" engine seemed like it was going to hold together...it sounded like a typical SBC V8 and the 3-speed and entire drive train didn't have any unusual noises or growls...we might make it to Des Moines anyway.

Four hours later, it was starting to get dark as we went through North Platte, Nebraska, and deciding we had enough light, and time, to get to Kearney, another 100 miles up the road, we'd stay over-night there. That would put us more than halfway to Omaha...we'd been making good time. The '57 was running okay and the radiator we put in was doing its job...the car wasn't overheating. As darkness settled, we had about 14 miles to go, find a motel and do the rest of the trip tomorrow.

I'd been worried about the electrical system, seeing as how the old generator was still on the car...and the fact that we'd had to re-do all the wiring inside the steering column to get brake lights and running lights. When we got the car, it didn't have park lights, turn signals or brake lights...we couldn't figure out why until we pulled the steering wheel only to discover there was no turn signal canceller or wiring to the brake switch. I guess the previous owner needed it worse than the car did...or something like that.

Well, nothing to do but find out if it's going to work the way it's supposed to, I pulled on the light switch.

They didn't....!!!

No headlights when I wiggled the switch...they'd worked in the garage.

"Uh-oh, now what?" Dan asked.

"Just keep going. Hopefully we can make Kearney before the cops see us running unlighted," I said. "Get a motel and see if we can figure out what's wrong with it there. Don't think there's much as far as auto parts stores or mechanics in these small towns."

Fortunately, the moon was coming out and the highway was moonlit...shouldn't be a problem getting to Kearney.

Unless the Highway Patrol spots us...

"Yep, look, right there," I pointed, "going the other direction."

"Think they saw us," Dan asked.

"No way of knowing," I answered...hoping the officer was looking somewhere else when we whizzed by.

Five minutes later I figured we were in the clear, they didn't see us. "Good, we'll make Kearney yet."

Nope, just then, red lights lit up my rear view mirror. Uh-oh...busted.

The female patrol officer was real nice...once we got stopped, she asked us why we were running without headlights. I explained, telling her we had no way to fix it out here. "Well, you certainly can't go any further on the Interstate without headlights. I can call a tow truck for you."

"I don't think we can have the car towed, it's too low, as you can see," I argued, "they'll never get a hook under it and it'll never get up on a ramp truck. Can't you just take us to the next exit and we'll see if we can call my brother..."

"Okay," she said.

I was shocked, didn't think she'd go for it.

"But, mind this," she ordered. "Don't go over 40 mph...and I'll be right behind you. Stay as far to the right as you can and take the first exit. It's two miles up the road."

Well, that first exit took us into Lexington, a very small town. We got off the Interstate and headed in, turned into the first motel we came to. Once we were in the motel parking lot and the trunk open, the highway patrol woman turned around and went back out on the Interstate. Fortunately, we didn't get a ticket or a warning…guess she felt sorry for us in that old ugly copper colored '57 Chevy.

We grabbed a room, asked the desk clerk if there was a parts store around. She said there was but they were closed, "…but I have his home number, I can call him."

The owner took the call, even came out to meet us at his store, only four blocks from the motel, he was a hot rodder, too. He opened up and we bought brushes for the generator. We tore it off in the parking lot, under the light and took it up to the room…"overhauled" it. In the morning, we put it back on and continued our journey.

On Sunday, at Des Moines, the generator again took a dump…this time it cooked the regulator, thought the car was on fire for a while. We borrowed a friend's car, went and got more brushes and a regulator. We couldn't get any of it to work together and neither could several friends…we ended up killing the battery…oh great…!!! Back to the parts store, bought a new one. On the advice of friends and their stories, they told us we could "drive forever" on the battery alone…didn't need to charge it. We weren't too sure about that, but what chance did we have to get back home, other than a very expensive tow?

We headed for home on Monday morn…and never turned the car off 'til we pulled into the garage…we kept the car running while we got gas, while we got lunch and while we got snacks. To help things, we didn't use the stereo…or headlights, on the whole trip home…we got home late afternoon, still in daylight, no need for headlights.

Let me add here, FWIW, we did find out the "ugly" '57 we now owned had been an ISCA show champion back in 1967-'69 and was built in Milwaukee, Wisconsin, by an upholsterer by the name of Don Gasjdoz (long ago passed on)…how it got to ColoRODo and its completely deteriorated state is another story entirely, perhaps for another time…

Shortly after we got home, we installed an alternator on the old 283"…that effectively solved one of our problems…but later that summer, after a trip to Rapid City, South Dakota, we encountered a larger problem, one that couldn't be fixed easily enough on the side of the road. However, that's not the end of this particular "incident"…

THE WASHINGTON INCIDENT

Here's the continuation of the three week trip to the west coast...beginning in Des Moines, Iowa. Oh yeah, before heading out, you should make certain your car is in good running order!

August, 1984. Washington State. In late July, we did a trip to Des Moines, Iowa, for the Leadsled Nats in our "new" radical "kustom." Some time before that, we'd planned on going to the Yakima Mini-Nats in Yakima, Washington, after the Leadsled Nats, and had already set our vacation plans...so what did we do? We drove the radical '57 back to Denver on Monday and put it in the garage...we tossed the dirty clothes into the hamper, figuring we'd take care of them when we got back...grabbed a bunch of clean t-shirts, clean underwear (didn't your Mom ever tell you to make sure you wore clean underwear? Mine sure did!) and the rest of the necessities we'd need, and loaded up our hot rods (me in my newly re-painted/upholstered '40 Studebaker coop and Dan in his two-toned '47 Chevy Aerosedan), filled the gas tanks and lit out for Yakima, by way of Utah, Nevada and California on Tuesday morn.

Once in Yakima, we unexpectedly met some of our friends from Casper, Wyoming, at the event...Rick and Lee Ann Thurston...they were driving their old stand-by --a black '48 Chevy sedan delivery...remember that Rick...??? We didn't know they'd be there and was surprised to see them. After pal-ing around with them for the weekend, we found out they were going to Seattle after the show...but first, they'd planned on doing some sight-seeing around Mt. Rainier... "Hey, we'll go with you, we have a few more days to kill and we'd planned on going to Seattle and then to Victoria, BC, while we're up here."

At the Yakima Mini-Nats award ceremony, Dan and I were awarded the "Long Distance" award...but had to explain that, in fact, we'd traveled 1300 miles farther than we'd needed to, since we started in Denver, Colorado, drove to Des Moines, Iowa, then back to

ROGER JETTER

- Automotive Art
- T-Shirt Designs
- Concepts

PO Box 440042, Aurora, CO 80044

303-690-4051

ROGER JETTER

Author/Freelancer

- Bangin' Gears & Bustin' Heads
- Fast Cars, 4-speeds & Fist-fights
- Recollections, Regrets, & Random Acts
- Accidents & Incidents
- Faded Thunder
- Arsenal Code R.E.D.
- Broke Down a Million Miles From Home

Denver and on to Yakima, Washington. I got into my first video at that event cuz I used to stick a sign in the window of my Studebaker poking fun at all those guys that put mega-dollar prices on their car at events. It read: "Very rare street rod with low miles- $85,000." The guy filming the video thought I was serious and offered me a "chance to sell your car via my video." Needless to say I was quite nervous if that's any consolation to that video guy if he's reading this…I'd bet most people that saw that video KNEW I was nutso to ask that kind of money for my "orphan."

After spending some sight-seeing time around Rainier and the area, we finally made it to Seattle and went to the Space Needle, the football stadium and down to the market next to the water. While there, Dan's '47 started acting up…hard to start, but in typical Seattle weather… drizzly and cool and we didn't want to do any mechanical work in the wet, so we planned on taking care of it later. After our tour of Seattle, we decided to go south to do some sight-seeing and take a trip around the Olympia Peninsula…we'd heard it was gorgeous around there (more on that later)…

We parted company with Rick and Lee Ann, with instructions on where to meet them in Victoria for the big shindig over there…seems it was some kind of anniversary celebration for the city.

Dan and I headed south to Tacoma and then Olympia…took Highway 101 up around the area…we thought we'd see some great scenery since the forest is so wet all the time and being the highway is right along the coast, figured we'd get some great views of the mountains, of the Strait of Juan De Fuca and the Pacific Ocean. Well, needless to say all we saw were very tall evergreens…on both sides of the highway…seldom did we see the ocean and never did see any of the Olympic Mountains…we drove all the way past Lake Crescent and gave up…we made a U-turn and headed back the way we came. Dan always has maps with him and suggested lightly that maybe we could take one of the ferries that plied the waters there over to Victoria, BC. Figured that'd be a real kick to put our hot rods on a ferry. We stopped in Port Angeles and checked availability…we were told the ferries were booked all day, so had them check availability for the next day…we were then informed the ferries were booked all week because of the big shindig in Victoria. Hmmmmmm, guess we're not going to meet Rick and Lee Ann in Victoria after all, and don't know if they ever made it there!

We ate lunch in Port Angeles trying to figure out our next direction. "According to my map, there's a ferry at Port Townsend, it may take us to Whidbey Island and we could avoid going back through Seattle, if they aren't booked solid," Dan offered. It didn't take long to get to Port Townsend…late that afternoon we boarded the ferry after waiting in line for over an hour…it took us about an hour to traverse the watery distance…as we were about to get off the ferry, Dan's car wouldn't start. "Oh great, here we are on a ferry and he can't get his car started…is his car destined to travel back and forth on the water forever?" Dan is panicked…everyone else behind us already has their cars running and are waiting. "Hurry, come on start….!!!" Dan ordered. I got out of my car, opened his hood to see if I can see any problem…is it flooded? Got spark? After grinding on it for what surely seemed like 35 minutes…it finally started. "I don't like that," Dan said, "what're we going to do?"

"Nothing right now…we need to get off this thing. I'm sure the ferry has a time-table they have to keep and we've just shortened it for them." Everyone waiting behind us was relieved we got "that old car" running…so was I! Bet they never wanted to see another "old car" on that ferry. Once we were back on solid pavement, we cruised on up through Oak Harbor on Highway 20… and across Deception Pass, and what a view that was. Deception Pass was named in 1792 by Captain George Vancouver because he was misled into thinking Whidbey Island was a peninsula…and he was looking for a safe harbor for his ships. The highway took us across two bridges…I'd never been on a steel span bridge that had an island in the middle of it. I later found out that Deception Pass connects Whidbey Island to Fidalgo Island and is 180 feet above the Strait of Juan De Fuca (see, we got to see the Strait anyway…we just went in the wrong direction). On one side of the small island is narrow Canoe Pass and that bridge span is 511 feet long. The other side is known as Deception Pass and that span is 975 feet long. The bridge span is actually breathtaking from the beaches below and it's one of

Washington State's scenic wonders. Most amazing is the bridge and span were dedicated in 1935, it's not new at all...it's older than I am.

"Car running fine now?" I asked Dan via the CB as we drove past the span.

"Seems to be," Dan said, " looks like we'll need the Interstate at Burlington to go north, maybe get some petrol somewhere soon." We stopped for fuel in Bellingham, turned the cars off at the pumps and, yep, you guessed it. Dan's '47 would not start...now what? After checking everything we could I decided it was the points. I pulled the cap off and watched as he cranked it over...points didn't even open. Yep, there's the problem. "Okay. What do we do now? How do we solve the problem and keep going?" Dan asked.

"New points," I said, "and look, there's a parts store right across the street."

We changed the points and condenser right there in the gas station lot. It took us about 45 minutes to get them changed cuz the engine and everything else was hot...I "tuned" the engine by ear (burnt it too...!!!). By that time it was late afternoon but we continued on...headed for Hope, BC, the "famous" (infamous?) town that Sly Stallone blew up in his first Rambo movie and we were looking forward to touring in Canada. But, that's not the end of this trip...

THE CANADIAN INCIDENT

Own a radar detector? We did and learned not to trust it. This incident is a continuation of the previous story and a continuation of our three week vacation.

August, 1984. Western Canada. After the car trouble in Bellingham and getting Dan's '47 Aerosedan running, we headed to Canada. Just before we got to the Canadian border, we'd stopped in Lynden -- needed Canadian money...couple hundred ought to do it for the day or two we'd planned on being there.

At the International gate between the U.S. and Canada, the RCMP officer asked us what our plans were for entering Canada, how long we were staying and "what kind of cars are you driving?" He wasn't a hot rod fan, his guesses were way off and in minutes we were on our way.

We planned on spending the night in Hope, BC, but didn't make it that day, what with Dan's points problem...we made Chilliwack and spent the night there. Next morning, while eating breakfast in a local restaurant, several people checked out our cars and approached us, asked if we were there for the car show coming up that weekend. Said "No, we're headed home, don't know anything about their show." The next question was "Why did you come to Canada then?" We simply said "sight-seeing."

We were anxious to get to Hope but 85 kilometers an hour was slow...felt like we were hardly moving...and my speedo read 55 mph! Ha...1984...remember that? The US government was keeping a lid on speed...making sure we weren't going to kill ourselves with excessive speed, or waste gasoline they said was going to run out! Didn't really expect Canada to have the same speed limit, but they did ...couldn't make much time at 55 going anywhere in the US...so, before we left Denver, we'd bought a radar detector to enable us to run just a "bit" faster than the law would like...or allow, anyway.

Figured we'd never cover the amount of miles we wanted to on our trip at 55 mph.

Arriving in Hope mid-morning, we drove around looking for all the things we could remember in Sly Stallone's first "Rambo" movie - - the steel bridge outside of town, the gas station that was blown up, the Sheriff's office that was destroyed…Hope was a nice small town in the Canadian mountains…and a nice place to live I'd bet. After we'd seen most all the "props" in Hope, we hit the highway again.

It was mid-afternoon when the clouds began to look menacing on Highway 3, headed south and east, a lot like the low clouds in the Rambo movie, very appropriate for us. Figured it was going to cut loose and rain but we drove out of it. We traveled through a couple of Provincial Parks, through beautiful mountains when we noticed one park sign that had a great waterfall (cannot remember the name though). It was time for a soda break anyway. The falls were about a half a mile off the parking area…we decided to hike up. We met a couple of guys coming down, both had backpacks and both wore t-shirts that read: "Bears-one, People-zero." We stopped them and asked what that was about, told us they had an encounter with a bear in their tent last month while they were camping in another park …the bear had almost broken one guy's arm standing on it inside the tent looking for food and said he almost bit his tongue off to keep from screaming in pain. Both guys played dead hoping the bear would leave as quickly as it entered their tent. Fortunately it did and both guys thanked their lucky stars for their lives.

Leaving the falls, I couldn't take 85 kilometers an hour any more…told Dan to "turn on the radar and let's make time." We'd installed the radar detector in Dan's '47, just below the top of the windshield, since he usually ran the front door most of the time…well, OK, all the time cuz he's great at reading a map…remember, this is way before GPS's. Besides, I liked to follow and check out scenery…

We were in the third week of our trip and had 6 days to get home from the Northwest. Past Princeton the highway was good so I kicked the speed up. When we left the Provincial Park, I'd left first and Dan followed. I caught a group of eight cars and followed, for a while…needless to say, 85 kilometers an hour was too pokey. "I'm going around Dan, don't wanna follow any more." A long straight stretch of highway appeared, going uphill, but that's okay cuz my Studey had plenty of 400" SBC power. "Follow me," I called over the CB, "no one coming, clean shot." I goosed the Stude past 85 kilometers. One down, two down, past three and the Studey's speedo was reading 90mph (no idea how many kilometers that was)…Dan was behind me. I had lots of pedal to go, lots of straight highway ahead and no one coming at us.

"Rog," Dan yelled, urgency in his voice. "The radar detector's going off…fast…means a cop is close."

"Don't see anything," I answered, passing numbers four and five.

"I'm slowing. I'm running over 90," Dan said. "We'll get a ticket."

"Don't slow. If you do, we'll get separated. Kick it in the butt, stay with me…it's still clear. I'll tell you when to slow or slide between cars." I'd just passed numbers six and seven…the speedo edged closer to 100…one more to go.

"These people will think we're nuts," Dan said.

"So what? We're from the U.S., we are crazy. Crazy Americans. C'mon, one more car to pass, then free sailing. No more following at 55." Dan hung with me, all the time protesting the detector was screaming and his speedo was going to twist off. "I can't see a cop anywhere, or coming at us," I said, glancing at my speedo, reading 100 even. Number eight passed, I swung back into my lane. "Besides, if he's behind us, he'll have to wade through all the cars we just did…and this straight stretch of road can't last forever. I am not pulling over to wait or get one of his tickets…never had a Canadian ticket…don't want one. Stay with me." He did and slipped into the lane behind me.

Just after Dan pulled in, the straight stretch of highway gave way to the top of the hill and there were curves on the way down. We slowed, drove into Osoyoos and went to a local bank to turn in our Canadian money…then took Highway 97 south to the U.S. border. Our eastward travel had taken us through some of the most beautiful scenery that we had encountered...Canada is as beautiful as the U,S. Oh, BTW, we never did see that Canadian Highway Patrolman.

South of Osoyoos, we stopped at the International gate and were asked almost the same questions as the RCMP did...but they knew what our cars were and we were on our way home, glad to be back in the U.S. Since we were in northern Washington State, we decided to go see the Grand Coulee Dam on the Columbia River.

From there we headed east toward Spokane to spend the night. The next morning we cruised over to Coeur d'Alene, Idaho, and the huge lake there. We only got as far as Bozeman, Montana, that day. In the morning we decided to "tour" Yellowstone...hadn't been there in a few years so figured why not...we entered the park at the west side and did a whirlwind one day "tour"... saw Old Faithful but had to wait about 50 minutes to see it "blow," we saw Yellowstone Falls 'fall' for about five minutes, drove past Yellowstone Lake to Inspiration Point and then we headed south towards Jackson.

During our "whirlwind tour," we became a rolling car show. When we stopped, tourists took pix of our hot rods instead of scenery...well, I guess we were part of the scenery. Most couldn't believe we'd actually driven the cars and were astounded at the ColoRODo plates -- if they only knew how far we'd already driven!

The sun was beginning to set and we hadn't even gotten through the Tetons...we thought we better find a motel in Jackson...but every motel in Jackson had "No Vacancy" signs lit. Uh-oh. Not much to do but go down the road...it was dark-thirty as the lights of Jackson grew dim in our rear view mirrors. Dan said the next town was 80 miles away..."and it's small...may not be a motel there." The two-lane appeared empty except for us...an hour later, I called Dan on the CB, said I was tired of driving mountain roads at 45-50 mph in the dark, besides it was close to midnight and to "find a rest area or a spot to stop." A motor home was parked in a view spot so we pulled in behind it..."Guess this is as good as it gets tonight." I said. Ever sleep in a car with no heater, in late August, in the mountains? It gets cold, down to 60 degrees! We didn't bring any jackets or carry blankets so we nearly froze...we awoke around 5:30 just as the dawn cast rays over the mountains...they always say that's the coldest time of the morning and "they" aren't kidding...I had to set on my fingers to keep them warm...makes it hard to drive that way! But drive we did... another hour took us to Pinedale...there was a small café already open and we rushed in smelling a nice warm breakfast and pots and pots of hot coffee...

By the time we were filled, the sun had warmed the day and we headed for Rock Springs, Wyoming...from Rock Springs, Denver, and home, was only another 380 miles – piece of cake for the miles we'd already put on our hot rods.

THE BLACK HILLS INCIDENT

An old '57 Chevy, an even older engine in it and problems with driving it. This incident occurred while we were on a three day weekend trip in a car we'd recently purchased from a used car lot.

April, 1985. South Dakota. Spring in ColoRODo...the days got warmer and the urge to get the hot rod out and go somewhere was itching the accelerator foot. But we had a ways to go... body work on the radical '57 wasn't quite done.

Whoa... let me back up...after our three week trip to the Northwest (August, 1984), we decided the kustom'57 Chevy needed serious body work - September, '84 we started removing concrete hard bondo - sanding the copper color (supposed to be Candy Tahitian Orange - according to a previous owner), we realized it'd take forever removing paint then primer to get to bondo...or most of the winter that was coming - days grew shorter and temps fell quickly. In ColoRODo, snow can fall any time after Labor Day so we hurried...reason being we were on the driveway of my condo –my Stude warm in my single car garage.

Mid-September, after sanding in the cold, I decided to see what "heat" would do to 20 year old bondo? I grabbed the propane torch and held it to the body...a scraper popped off big chunks. No more sanding, let's see what's underneath. As darkness settled in, out came the trouble light. Chris, my son, 13 at the time, held the propane torch. Dan, my bro, handled the scraper and I held the trouble light. We worked one panel at a time, peeled off bondo until my fingers froze!

With bare metal showing, I couldn't shoot primer without it freezing, I needed a new house...I'd been in my condo five years. I found the right house in March - with an attached two car garage and a huge back yard, someday there'd be a 30' x 40' back there...for the time being, the new garage gave warmth for stripping bondo.

By the end of March, we were close...but it was still cold enough I couldn't prime. In April, we'd decided to go the "Counts" rod run in

July, in the Black Hills...our goal - drive the car in primer. Every weeknight and weekend thereafter was devoted to body work...by June, most of the car was in primer...we then worried about the engine again. It was still the same old tired 283". We'd replaced the generator with an alternator, installed a new fuel pump and re-gasketed everything – no more leaks. We cleaned under the hood and did a rattle can engine "rebuild"...good enough for the girls we went out with (NOT...!!!). We installed Olds swivel buckets, the kind that lock into place, something the car didn't have when we drove it off the used car lot. With the interior tidied up, we masked it and shot gray primer. But, it lacked something – the one thing every kustom needs - a name. I studied it - it was low and looked sneaky...I named it "Street Sneaker." I found a pair of my son's old baby sneakers and attached the laces to the underside of the trunk and let them hang down over the full width taillights – perfect.

July 4th, the car was ready for its debut, at a local rod run...everyone liked it but there was something missing. It looked massive in gray primer, like a Navy battleship. Since all the trim had been removed in 1964-1966, it was naked. We needed graphics, or flames. I grabbed the masking tape, laid out some designs. Dan came over, liked what he saw, together we did scallops.

Color? Uhm...what do we have? Plenty of shake n' shoot to choose from. We finally settled on a dark green. The scallops really changed the appearance.

In mid-July, the car was as "done" as we were going to get it. We tossed our suitcases into the trunk on Friday and headed for Rapid City, 400 miles/six hours away. We took I-25 north past Cheyenne headed for Chugwater. What? Gotta check out a town named "Chugwater," Wyoming. Not much there- a quaint little tavern, Lewis & Clark probably opened it, several log buildings, a couple of ancient storefronts and a post office.

Historians believe "Chugwater" is derived from a Mandan bison hunt - a chief was disabled during the hunt and his son took charge. Under his direction, Indians (oooops - PC: Native Americans) drove bison over nearby cliffs. When the buffalo hit the ground, "chugging" was heard. Since a stream was near the cliffs, the site of the stampede was "the place with water where the buffalo chug." Sad to say, Chugwater Creek is dry and no there were no buffalo skeletons that I could see.

North of Chugwater, we grabbed a two-lane and headed east to Lusk, Wyoming. After lunch, we checked fuel and water, added oil...all was fine.

We crossed the South Dakota line...Dan wanted pics in front of the "Welcome to" sign. As I slowed, I heard a distinct sound coming from the engine...wasn't good. After pictures, we continued ...our motel and the Counts rod run wasn't much farther, but the ol' '57 wasn't sounding good as I coasted down the long hill, As I pulled in to the motel, sounded like one rod was about to go - there was serious knocking. I told Dan "this road trip was done - the '57 wouldn't make it home under its own power."

The event was held in the motel's back lot, there was no need to drive the car. We had a great time and had friends confirm my diagnosis after I'd started it several times. Sunday we'd secured a trailer ride home...our "new" friend, Lynn Finlayson, Alliance, Nebraska, had trailered his shoebox "Ranchero"...he offered to take the '57, and us, back to Denver.

We loaded the '57, Dan rode with Lynn in his El Camino pulling the trailered '57, Chris and I drove Lynn's "Ranchero," and that was an experience in itself...by 7PM Sunday evening, we arrived at Lynn's home. He took the time to show us his projects and all his collectibles.

Denver was still four hours away, it was late and we had another problem - how to fit four in an El Camino? Quite simply, can't! I refused to ride in the El Camino bed even though it was a warm July evening. Chris and I climbed into the '57, Dan rode with Lynn to give him directions. It was fun, sitting in the driver's seat, window down, breeze blowing and not having to worry about watching the road...looking out over the top of the El Camino for a different view.

We arrived home after midnight and unloaded and pushed the '57 into the garage...it'd be another six months before we rebuilt a 350" engine...by Spring, 1986, the bodywork on the car had been refinished in my two car garage because I insulated the garage heavily, added wallboard and a heater – we worked in shirt sleeves.

We drove the car in primer for several years while doing small things to it. In 1989, we had our good friend, Ed Overholt, do the finish bodywork. Later it was painted Mint Green and re-named "Hint of Mint II," a nod to the original name in 1967... after that, it was upholstered and went back to its winning ways, earning more awards, trophies, cash prizes and paid appearances than it ever did when it did the ISCA show circuit in 1967-'69.

THE GASOLINE INCIDENT!

When the fuel gauge shows a quarter of a tank left, better heed its warning and find a gas station NOW! This incident occurred while we were on our way home from St Paul, Minnesota.

August, 1985. Eastern ColoRODo. I bought a '57 Chevy in 1972... a 210 two door, had a smashed up front clip...built it - three times over 30 years - first as a resto (1972) - six cylinder and primered. Drove it that way for two years, then redid it (1974) - Pearl White, brown flames, nosed/ decked, '54 Chevy grille, '57 wagon rear bumper, white vinyl interior, plaid fabric inserts, brown carpet, chrome reversed wheels/moons...a 'sled' in a 'hot rod' world. The last re-do was in 1986...this time everything was painted Dove Gray including outside windshield trim and rear window trim, a widened Maverick rear bumper (w/rolled pan) between dual stacked 80's Corvette taillights, modified front bumper w/air dam, flat aluminum bar grille, five spoke wheels and body mods. For accent on the Dove Gray paint, I added pink and blue graphics on the sides and asymmetrical graphics on the hood. The interior was gray velour over Chevy SS buckets, with the same graphics through them and headliner, only done in fabric. The console/dash/window moldings were gray leather and it was powered by a 400" SBC/ T-400 tranny...that iteration won countless awards over the 15 years I drove it all over the U.S. – I eventually sold that '57 in 2001.

Anyway, the point of this is the gas gauge in a '57 Chevy is not entirely accurate (don't know if that's true to all '57's, but it sure was to all thirty of them I've owned!) When the tank was full, it read three-quarters...needless to say, when it read empty...it was as dry as the Sahara...!!!

In 1981, the Pearl White lacquer began checking badly, sun had dry-rotted the interior (it sat outside summers and winters) and the six cylinder was getting tired. A friend in my Iowa home town had just opened a body shop...I asked if he wanted to do the customizing, body work, paint and engine work…"Sure, bring it back." Could be a "calling card custom" for his business…

I hauled it back, along with illustrations of how I wanted the car to look, expecting top notch custom work.

Sadly, it never got started on. It sat outside in cold, snowy Iowa winters and hot, humid summers for four years…and no surprise, parts came up missing…I'd bet the guys that patronized the midnight auto supply were sad to see it leave.

In 1985, Dan and I planned on the St. Paul, Minnesota Nats. I drove my '40 Studebaker and Dan drove his '47 Chevy Aerosedan. Figured it'd be an ideal time to bring the car back to Denver. Our Iowa home town was on the way and we'd do the same on the return so we purchased a tow bar…the kind that hooked to bumpers…dropped it off at Mom's place on the way.

On Monday, back from St. Paul, we went to my pal's body shop, cut weeds, chased away snakes and spiders, kicked out several mice and evicted hordes of wasps from the '57. Front bumper and bolts were still in the trunk where I'd stored 'em four years previous. We reassembled it, put it on…and bolted the tow bar to the bumper of my '40 Studebaker and backed up to the '57, attached both together…once out on the street, we tossed headers, radiator, manifold on the back seat and then wheeled out the new 400" SBC I had shipped to Iowa, set it in the trunk, upside down, on the heads…tied it down good so it wouldn't move and closed the trunk.

Tuesday morn, we headed for Denver - 650 miles away.

Can you imagine a two-toned red and cream '47 Chevy (Dan's) leading a lime green 1940 Studebaker towing a decrepit white '57 Chevy? Quite a sight.

The '57 followed well…I was surprised, even more at the Stude's rear bumper being strong enough to handle the tow bar and the '57. At speed on I-80, most times I didn't even know the '57 was behind me. However, the Stude's gas mileage suffered.

We made good time, better than anticipated and when we were close enough to home, decided to take a short cut instead of going all the way into Denver on the Interstate and then back east to my home…we took Bromley Lane off the Interstate to Tower Road.

Remember, this was 1985, years before the city of Denver decided to build Denver International Airport ...there was absolutely nothing but 16 miles of straight south two-lane county road, no businesses at all and Tower Road would finally end at Colfax Avenue (the longest main street in the U.S).

Ten miles from Colfax, motoring along at 55 when...guess what...??? Yep, out of gas in the Stude (I swear the '57's gas gauge morphed into my Stude's dash!). Worse...neither of us carried extra gas. Dan was elected to go to town, 20 miles round trip, to get fuel...or tow the whole shootin' match to the station...??? Dan said tow, I said "That Aerosedan up to it?"

Now if we thought one rod towing a '57 Chevy, being led by another rod, was strange, can you now imagine a rod towing a rod towing a '57 Chevy? Wish I had a pic of that. When Dan pulled up next to the pumps, he ran out of gas that exact minute!

Even though this happened to the Stude, as I was towing the '57, it was portent of things...running out of gas happened many times in the gray '57 after the rebuild of the entire car for the third time: Outside Lincoln, Nebraska (1988), 5 miles from town, Dan towed me. Going to the Davenport, Iowa, KKOA event (1989), ran out in Iowa's Amana Colonies, Dan had to find the local station. On our way to Logan, Utah, for the Cache Valley Cruise (1993)...bought some crappy gas in Rock Springs, Wyoming...ran out near Big Bear Lake - Dan had to go find gas. Coming back from the Americruise in Peoria, Illinois (1994), ran out near Atlantic, Iowa, Dan towed me about 8 miles. You'd have thought we'd wise up and carry a gallon can...no...we didn't think about it til we were on the road.

Dan always seemed to have to find gas for me. He finally got back at me ... one hot afternoon in Southeast ColoRODo, running Highway 287, 18 miles south of Lamar, July, 2001. We'd been to Hugoton, Kansas, rod run, heading home- another 220 miles. Dan was driving my gray '57 and I was driving the radical kustom '57. He said he was getting low on fuel, "this gauge says it's empty and you told me when it's not bouncing, it's done, right?" I confirmed that...sure enough, just before the top of a hill, Dan radioed he was done. He coasted off the road. I drove to Lamar, 18 miles distant, bought a five gallon can and filled it while Dan sweated in the hot sun on the highway, then drove 18 miles back. In the meantime a CHP officer stopped and asked Dan what his problem was...the officer offered a gallon, but Dan declined knowing I was headed back.

Within the last couple of years, we both wised up...we each carry two gallon cans... it comes in handy, not only for he and I, but for some other friends we went rod running with...right Kerry? Right Phil? Right Ron?

THE VOLCANO INCIDENT

Talk about spur-of-the-moment side trips, this incident was unscheduled and still the best of our past trips. We were on a northwestern states rod running vacation.

August, 1986. Southern Washington State. The devastation was unimaginable - destruction & annihilation of life - total and complete. The sight we saw in contrast to green forest we'd driven through. Old growth pines flattened, laying the same direction, stripped bare, scorched black - victim of Mt. St. Helens! The volcano's pyroclastic flow (gas, steam, pulverized rock) had swept down the mountainside near 670 mph, hugging terrain, ending six miles from the crater. 1,500 degree temps evaporated anything less than trees.

Days earlier we'd enjoyed the Western Nats in Salem, visited my Uncle - conversation drifted from rods to sightseeing. He suggested Mt. St. Helens - it'd been six years since the 1980 eruption – he'd heard roads were open near the crater of the only active volcano in the continental United States. "Be careful," he cautioned, "those are logging tracks - dirt, gravel, narrow."

Didn't bother us, gravel roads were do-able and we'd already logged 1200 miles from Denver, ColoRODo. We hadn't planned on seeing a live volcano but were curious about what havoc one could wreak – a once-in-a-lifetime experience.

Driving in from Oregon, it was hard to believe there was a smoking volcano near. Pines lined both sides of the highway, breeze carried pine and wildflower scent and the sky was Azure blue. My son, Chris, and I were in my Studebaker, following my bro in his Chevy - our rod-running/vacation…no trailers used… getting there is half the fun. Our cars become attractions at tourist attractions.

The gray, dusty road took us through a valley. Mt. St. Helens' lower slopes were covered with a grayish 'blanket,' appearing like a "moonscape" of tan and off-white tones. The road edged dangerously close to a drop-off, we stopped and saw a hulk of a car. Wondered why it was there and hiked down.

In places, the road was graded below the level of ash - two/three feet deep, looked like freshly fallen snow, settled exactly like ColoRODo's powder snow. Higher up on the roadway we viewed Spirit Lake...not serene, placid waters you'd expect, but choked with floating trees. At the lake's north end, the barren face of a mountain commanded our gaze, showing an impossible 'high-water mark'. Below that mark, not a tree or bush grew, much less dirt! We learned the release of the Mt. St. Helens landslide (8000 million tons of rock and dirt) instantly raised Spirit Lake 207 feet, initiating a cataclysmic Tsunami that surged through the lake, pushed water up the side of the mountain for 820 feet. The force of the water rushing up, then back down, was more concentrated than the greatest ocean Tsunami. What didn't get torn off as Spirit Lake went up, got removed as the water receded.

We'd entered Washington via I-5 out of Portland and exited onto a two-lane, Mt. St. Helens was 60 miles farther. The road followed a river and we crossed it several times. From its cleanliness, we didn't know it carried flood waters, known as a Lahar. The eruption's heated ash cloud caused the instant melt of permanent snow on the mountain, liquefying it. The "flood" raced down the river bed at nearly 100 mph, gathering debris to a height of 60 feet, taking everything with it.

Every few miles along the highway we'd spot a sign: 'Tour Mt. St. Helens from the Air.' The CB crackled after the fourth. "Hey Rog, see those?"

"Could be fun," I answered. My son, 13 at the time, thought so, too. Of course, he's up for anything other than riding.

Several miles later, the final sign appeared, 'Air Tour, one mile ahead, turn right, go three miles.'

"Don't see prices."

"Can't cost that much." I said. "It's way out here, away from civilization, not many cars on this highway."

Right turn onto a mid-western style lane -- rutted, narrow, not well traveled. Tall pine trees lined both sides of the lane. Three miles slowly, took forever.

"If there's an airstrip in here, it's short," Dan said.

Soon we pulled into a large clearing. To the left of the lane, 75 yards ahead, parked under the tall pines, sat a vintage 1940's airplane, not looking very airworthy.

Dan surveyed the plane. "That old thing couldn't fly anymore?"

"Doesn't look like it's flown in ages."

A mobile home sat in front of the plane. On the other side of the dead-ended lane - a dilapidated shed. Wood weathered white, board ends pulled loose, nails rusting, mute testimony to the power of water, sun and time. "Plane would fare better in the shed, out of the weather, than under those pines," I remarked.

The airfield looked green, smooth, short! A woman exited the mobile home 'office', we exchanged pleasantries, asked about the ride. "Takes two hours. The pilot will fly you around the volcano and directly over the cone, it's only 15 miles north. $30 each." I pulled out $60 for Chris and I.

"Uhmmm, NO!" Dan said. "Don't feel like flying."

"What? Won't be any fun without you. Besides, you've got the camera."

The situation worsened, heated words exchanged, no other reason given. Couldn't understand his about-face. No amount of persuasion helped.

Bummer... back into the cars, disappointment setting in, saw it in my son's eyes. He finally broke the silence, holding back tears. "Would've been fun."

Why should I let my brother put a damper on it? "Okay, Bud, we'll go, Dan can wait." His face lit up.

I grabbed the mic, "Make a U-turn, Dan. Chris and I are going flying!" Minutes later I plunked down $60. Dan still refused.

"You sure?" The woman asked. "I'll have the pilot bring the plane, you two wait by the lane until it gets warmed up."

Consternation covered Dan's face. "You sure you want to fly in that thing?" He motioned blindly toward that vintage 1940's plane.

"Gotta be flyable," I tried to ease his mind...and mine. "Wouldn't sell rides if it were dangerous. The FAA would make sure of that."

An engine roared to life, Dan looked at me, surprised. "Sounds good."

We waited - the mobile home in front of us - couldn't see the vintage plane.

"Maybe they put a newer engine in that old plane, like we put V8's in our old cars, make 'em hot rods, maybe that old plane is hot rodded."

Before Dan answered, as we were watching the left side of the lane expecting the vintage plane to appear, out from behind the dilapidated shed on the right rolled a shiny new red and white Bonanza. The pilot taxied up, turned around...motioned Chris and I in...I looked at Dan. He ran toward the mobile home, yelling, struggling to find cash in his pockets.

We had a great ride. The pilot flew over the central cone three times, each time lower, over Spirit Lake and around the volcano twice. The view from above was awesome, the pilot's narrative made the flight special. It lasted three hours. Dan shot three rolls of film - great photos of Mt. St. Helens "from the air."

Two important things were learned that day...

First: NEVER assume. ASK! Then ask again!

Second: NEVER judge a book by its cover! Dan was certain that vintage plane sitting beside the airstrip was the one we were to fly in, he wasn't about to chance a trip in it. From that day forward, Dan always asks questions.

THE HOOD INCIDENT

After driving logging dirt roads, checking out a live volcano and an incredible airplane tour, what could possibly go wrong after that? This is the continuation of the previous story, from Mt. St. Helens and headed home in the second week of our vacation.

August, 1986. Broadus, Montana. We'd decided to go see where George made his last stand since it was "sorta" on the way to the Counts of the Cobblestone rod run...Sunday, we'd head home - Rapid City is 400 miles from Denver – a short 6 hour trip.

We over-nighted in Billings, drove to the Little Bighorn Battlefield National Monument (Custer Battlefield), south of Hardin, Montana. Arrived there early and after looking at all the artifacts/history it was noon. If we were to make Rapid by nightfall, we had to go.

We left the Monument, me in my '40 Stude, Dan his '47 Chevy and I asked, via the CB how the gas situation was. "Enough for another hundred miles," Dan said, looking at his maps. He likes different sight-seeing routes, he'd found a two-lane across the prairie to Belle Fourche, South Dakota. We'd get fuel in Broadus, ninety miles distance.

Keep in mind this trip was in 1986...we'd do a vacation like this for about $100 a day, all inclusive – food, fuel, motel. Can't do that anymore – motel costs $90-140.00 a night and fuel around $60.00 a stop - depending on how big the tank is and how far you want to drive in a day.

Bought gas in Broadus, plus a snack and an iced soda - no A/C in our rods. The wind had picked up and it was a blast furnace coming in the windows. Heading southeast, there were no other cars out there, we ran seventy mph on the two-lane. The wind got stronger as the day got shorter. South of Broadus we crested a hill, a long straight stretch of highway downward into a headwind, dirt and weeds flying at us. I was following Dan as I usually do...for just a second, I saw Dan's brake lights come on…I'm a ways back but I see his brake lights illuminate again…what's he doing? Dozing? Wind blow dirt in his eyes? I knew his windows were down. When he crossed the yellow center line I reached for the CB, "What're you doing?" He slowed. I finally see it…his hood has flown up and it's blocking the windshield. "Hold on to it," I yelled over the CB… "hold the steering wheel straight, I'll guide you." He was tapping the brakes and weaving all over the road…he told me the only area he could see out of was the three inch space between the bottom of the hood and the dash…not much area to keep a car on the road and get it stopped from 70, but he finally slowed and pulled onto the shoulder. Fortunately, there were no cars coming at him - might've been bigger trouble.

I stopped behind him, he got out of his car – shaken, he leaned against the car. "Wow…!!! Some wild ride. Didn't expect that. Happened fast, couldn't do anything. I noticed the hood bounce a time or two and then it just flew up. I was trying to get the hood to go back down by tapping the brakes but the wind is too strong."

"Hood is toast now," I said looking at the bends. "How's the windshield?"

"Glass didn't break."

"Let's see if we can get it back down." We both grabbed and pulled…hinges groaned and squealed, didn't want to move - both hinges were nearly pulled off the cowl, welds broken. We stopped pulling. Dan grabbed a hammer out of the trunk. "What're you doing?" I asked.

"Making it fit," he said, and proceeded to hammer the hinges. "Makes no difference on the paint, or the hinges now." It took some pulling, hammering, forcing and cursing, but we got it closed…didn't fit well and we needed to latch it. Dan grabbed the front and pulled, the latch pin dropped in. "Will it open?" I asked, "you'll need to check oil, tranny when we get to Rapid." I reached inside and pulled the release, Dan pulled the hood forward and up. "It'll open but won't stay latched," Dan said. "Need something to hold it down."

He grabbed some Instant Roadside Repair Wire out of his toolbox and wired the hood to the grille…not the coolest roadside repair, but it'd hold til we got to Rapid and have time to do more hammering and "fitting" for the final ride home.

It took a few hours to get to Rapid and the Counts rod run. We found our motel and started cleaning bugs off…while cleaning the interior, Dan found that all the nickels he'd won at the Jackpot, Nevada, casino on our way to Salem, had spilled because of his panic stop…I'd bet the car still has nickels rolling around under the seat. At the event, Dan almost won the 'Hard Luck' award, but lost to someone that lunched a tranny.

At the motel that night, I'd been thinking the same thing could happen to my hood. Fortunately, I was able to remove the hood's side panels from my Stude…I did that and closed the hood, took some Instant Roadside Repair Wire, wrapped it around the underside hood support and twisted that around the radiator supports. It held and once home I fixed it permanently…you'll read about that shortly.

We had a great time at the Counts rod run, did a lot of explaining how the hood on Dan's Chevy got bent and did some sightseeing around Rapid City, particularly the South Dakota Air & Space Museum at Ellsworth Air Force Base, 10 miles east of Rapid, home of the U.S. B-1 bombers.

Couple weeks later, home in Denver, we found a complete '47 Chevy Aerosedan parts car advertised locally, paid $150.00 and dismantled it. Dan decided at the rod run his resto-stocker look just wasn't cutting it anymore…it needed mods…we welded the center piece to the hood, making it one piece, then stripped the paint and sent it to Sam Jamison for louvers. We pulled off the 'parts' trunk, stripped it, removed the inner structure and punched that full of holes, too. We sunk a license plate box and a third brake light in. Dan's car was acrylic enamel paint and had paint left from his initial paint job so we sprayed the hood and trunk in my garage. It matched well enough that no one ever knew it had been damaged. The mods changed the look of his car.

Now here's the moral of this story (and the permanent "fix" I said I'd let you in on) : Never trust a secondary hood latch…too many times on these old cars, someone has adjusted it too many times and it simply won't catch anymore, or it's been removed cuz they couldn't adjust it correctly in the first place. Ever since that incident, both of us use an old Chevy U-joint (U-shaped bolt) and cable or chain from the hood to the pan with a Chevy U-bolt there too, and a small padlock as the secondary latch...we simply don't trust a hood that is not locked down anymore, besides, it keeps unwanted fingers from under the hood. We've never had another incident with any of our hoods since.

THE VERY LARGE ARRAY INCIDENT

The White Mountains of Arizona are famous for alien abduction stories. The VLA is a series of radio telescopes situated east of the White Mountains and just outside of Magdalena, New Mexico. No, we didn't get abducted but weren't entirely certain aliens didn't cause our breakdown!

October, 1988. Socorro, New Mexico. Off to Lake Havasu, Arizona for the "Run to the Sun" event held on the London Bridge Resort golf course.

I was driving the '40 Studebaker coop and Dan was driving his '47 Chevy Aerosedan. We headed south for Trinidad, Colorado and Raton Pass. Our first stop was to be in Carlsbad, to visit the world famous caverns. Since we were making this trip a mini-vacation, we weren't in a hurry to get to Lake Havasu. We arrived in Carlsbad and found a motel, we'd tour the caverns in the morning. To say the size of the cave opening is huge would be an understatement...I think you could fly a 747 into it and still have room. The caverns were cool despite the summer heat outside and the limestone had some great colors on them.

We spent most of the day there and when we left, cut across the New Mexico desert headed for Alamagordo as our destination for the night. Since we were so close to the White Sands National monument, we decided to take a drive out to it. From a distance, the white sands actually looked like snow...strange to see snow in the middle of the desert and once we were driving in them, the heat added to the confusion. Some of the larger dunes were 25-30 feet high and of course, drifted just like snow. The white sands stretched as far as the eye could see.

As we headed west toward Socorro from there, Dan reminded me that the VLA, the Very Large Array of radio telescopes wasn't far from Socorro...better go check those out too. Somewhere between Carrizozo and Socorro, Dan's '47 broke a driver's side rear shock

63

mount...only he didn't know it til we got to the motel. Probably wouldn't have noticed it if I hadn't been following him. Where are we going to find a '57 Chevy rear shock in Socorro, NM? There weren't any junkyards in the area so the next best thing was to find someone to weld it. Fortunately, we were told there was a farm equipment shop on the south side of town. We drove down, walked in and talked to the guy inside. We told him of our problem and he said "If you get it off the car I can weld it. Won't do it on the car-too close to the gas tank." Back to the motel to remove the shock. We placed the small jack we carry under the leaf spring to hold it in place and removed the u-bolts. The broken piece was still attached to the shock so we took both pieces down to the shop. It didn't take but a few minutes to have it welded back together, making sure to keep it straight so the shock would fit back on without any problems. It actually took longer to remove and replace it than it did to heal it up. After the piece cooled off enough we put it back under the car and hooked the shock to it. We'd hoped it would stay together for the duration of the trip...it did and stayed on right up until 2014, when Dan sold his '47 Chevy. As far as we know, the welded bracket is still on the car...welded good.

The next morning we headed for the VLA, it was only about 30 miles west of Socorro and up on the Plains of San Augustin. There are 27 radio telescopes and each telescope dish is 82 feet across, weigh 230 tons each, can be moved on railroad tracks and can be spread across the plains in a "Y" pattern. The scientists can maneuver them around on the Plains so that they can be very far apart, or close together to concentrate the radio signals coming into the huge dishes. We took a self-guided tour of the grounds and the museum, seeing lots of pictures of far off galaxies in parts of our universe.

After spending quite a few hours there, we headed west up over the mountains towards Arizona. We stayed over-night in Eagar at the beginning of the White Mountains. The next morning we wound down through pines and mountains most of the day and dropped into the Salt River Canyon...the scenery was spectacular through there. Globe, Arizona, was really cool but the road was narrow and rough. From there we drove into east Phoenix, finding a motel along the way. The next morning we took a two lane out of Phoenix towards

Parker and our ultimate destination of Lake Havasu. As we headed west both Dan and I spotted two dark things in the distant sky. Looked like a couple of big birds at first until they got closer...and it didn't take long for them to get to us so we could see them plainly. No more than about hundred feet above us and coming straight at us were three fighter jets and they screamed right over the top of us...the roar of three jet engines drowned out everything-stereo, CB, road noise, engine noise...way loud at that height. We thought that was really neat but had no idea why they were so low and following the road. We watched in our side mirrors the best we could until they were gone. We were driving about 65 mph, talking about seeing them when we heard a dull roar that got much louder...scared us as the three jets made a pass over us, going the same direction we were. In a matter of seconds they were gone again and we never saw them after that. Dan and I speculated that they turned around to check out the two hot rods heading west on the lonely two-lane. Have no idea if they were military jets or privately owned but it was cool they were flying so low.

We had a great time at Lake Havasu's "Run to the Sun" event for three days. Nothing more happened on our way home but my old saying holds "If you can't fix your car on the side of the road, stay home!"

THE LONG BEACH INCIDENT

The ocean beckoned us, the big bridge broke us. This incident occurred while we were on a two week Fall vacation.

October, 1990. Long Beach, California. One more time, we decided to go to Lake Havasu for the rod run there. I drove the chopped '57, riding with me was my GF at the time Darlynn. Dan drove his '47 Chevy Aerosedan. After the Run to the Sun event in Lake Havasu, we decided to go to Los Angeles, Long Beach, to be exact, since my daughter was living there. The gal I was dating at the time had never seen an ocean, let alone the Pacific Ocean.

We'd gone south towards Parker, and Quartzite, Arizona to get on I-40. We crossed the Colorado River into California and across the desert. We stopped in the Joshua Tree National Park so we could see the cactus and then drove into Indio, Thousand Palms and Palm Springs. As we drove deeper into the valley, the horizon seemed to have a brown cast to it. The farther west we drove, the "foggier" it seemed to be and the closer we got to L.A., the worse it was. We finally deduced it was smog...and in L.A. it even smelled bad. Couldn't believe the traffic around there, mid-afternoon it was like rush hour in Denver. We finally found my daughter's home late afternoon. Melissa, my daughter, suggested we park both our cars in the garage since she thought they wouldn't be safe on the residential street over-night.

At my daughter's home, my gal friend asked if we could go as far west on land, by driving, as we could get. Tuesday morning, we set out to find that place. We took Seaside Boulevard and traveled a few miles before we could see a huge, tall bridge in the distance. As we drove up it, Darlynn suddenly got very nervous, I knew she didn't like heights and this bridge was high up in order to allow several sea-going large ships to pass under. Seaside Boulevard had turned into Harbor Freeway and on the down-side, the '57 developed a problem. I got on the CB and told Dan I had a problem, the car was starting to jerk and to find the nearest street or exit. The first exit went right into a corner gas station and I aimed for that. Just as I was turning off the highway, the car died and I coasted into a parking spot away from the pumps. As we got out of the car, Darlynn's face was white as a ghost. I asked if she liked the view from atop the bridge but she said all she saw was the floor of the '57. She would not look outside the car!

I tried to start the car again but it wouldn't turn over…wouldn't do anything, somewhere we lost spark. With the hood open we checked everything obvious-coil wire was still attached, points were okay, check the wires to the starter, they were as they should be, battery posts were cleaned in hopes that was it. Nope, maybe the coil died. Dan had a spare in his car so we tried that. Nope, wasn't it. Check for burnt wires next, maybe something is grounding out. Traced the wiring to the ignition and nothing is burnt. Even pulled out every fuse in the panel and checked them. What is it? Battery cable from trunk- mounted battery to starter was good and not torn or broken. After an hour of checking, we were kinda stumped, besides we were gathering a crowd and were trying to answer their questions as we were hunting the problem. Most wanted to know what kind of car we were driving simply because the Mint Green chopped '57 Chevy hardtop was so radically changed it wasn't recognizable. Others wanted to know where we were from and where we were going. Dan finally took the battery out of his car and swapped with mine…didn't help. Suggestions were coming from right and left among the people. We didn't have headlights, taillights, horn, stereo or CB-nothing worked!

What would cause a total loss of electrical power in a car? I decided to grab a flashlight to check the back of the instruments in the dash. Anything electrical was suspicious. The aftermarket gauges were the last to check because they were so far up in the dash they were hard to see. I finally get my head past the clutch and brake pedals, get the flashlight aimed in the right direction and then I saw it! The back of the after-market Ammeter gauge was all burnt, the plastic covering on the wires looked like they got really hot. Told Dan "think I've found the problem," asked him for a pair of wire cutters cuz I wasn't going to take the time to unbolt the ends. I cut the wire from both sides of the gauge terminals. I was still upside down under the dash and didn't want to get out so asked Dan for a piece of heavy wire about six inches long and some butt connectors cuz I know he always carries extra wire and connectors in his toolbox. It takes a few minutes to connect the two loose ends together cuz I can't get all my arms and hands behind the dash comfortably, but I get it done. Since I'm on my back, I ask Dan to pull the shifter out of gear to neutral and try the ignition. It fires instantly. Hooray! We got power again. Once I knew we had power, I pulled the ammeter gauge out of the dash and inspected it. It appeared that the connection between the two terminals fried itself and burnt in the middle, disconnected all power. I learned later that all Ammeter gauges will do that and are a fire hazard. When we got home, we replaced that gauge with a volt-meter.

However, that isn't the end of this story. That took us most of the day to sort out the problems and it was getting late. We hurried up the coast to LAX and the Dockweiler State Beach just west of the L.A. Airport, we'd gone as far west (according to the map) as we could get in Los Angeles and Darlynn waded in the ocean for a while. Just up the beach was a café near Playa Del Rey, we finally got some lunch, albeit a bit late. From there we went to the Hollywood Hills to see the huge Hollywood sign, then we hurried to Simi Valley to visit my uncle for a few hours and then headed out in the dark to find a motel for the night.

We spent a few more days sightseeing in L.A., spent a whole day at Disneyland and then headed for home. We drove to Las Vegas, spent the night there and visited a few casinos. The next day we drove all the way to Denver-a long day but happy to get home. I replaced the gauge the next week and checked the wiring again. To this day we have never had trouble with the Voltmeter and will never ever again use an Ammeter. It all goes back to the old saying I use: If you can't fix your car on the side of the road, better stay home. NOPE, NOT US...!!!

THE HOLLAND INCIDENT

Lost. Found. Broke down. Rained on! We were lucky on this one in that it only cost us an extra day on the road and hardly any cash outlay!

July, 1992. Southern Michigan. LOST! On dark, partially lit streets in the depths of Holland.

We'd gone for a cruise, got so turned around that east felt like north, south felt like west...we were lost and it was late.

We couldn't find a major thoroughfare, we drove around trying to find a major street we could take north, or south, or east, or maybe even west.

Okay, now that you're aware we were hopelessly lost and completely disoriented, let's back up a bit - I'll tell you how that happened.

Dan and I had headed east in our kustoms...me in the gray '57 Chevy and Dan driving the radical '57 Chevy hardtop. We left Denver early- first stop was our Iowa hometown to see Mom, then a short trip the next day, for the KKOA kustom show. The drive to Chicago was shorter than we figured, gave us an extra day to get to Holland (see, you thought we were lost in Holland, the country, dintcha...???) I've never been out of the US, save a trip to Tijuana, and Canada (eastern and western) and I can safely say there's plenty of sights to see in this country. Anyway, we arrived Chicago, rented a motel and decided to check out the "Cruising McDonald's" somewhere downtown. We asked around...finally got directions and drove downtown...found it but missed the cruise by one day. Oh well...back to the motel-it's late, we'll sightsee the city tomorrow. In the morning, we called car rentals...left the kustoms car-covered in the motel (with permission) and went to Sears Tower, (all the way to the top), drove Lake Shore Drive, past Soldier Field and out to Wrigley Field. It was a fun day, especially not having to worry about our kustoms. Since it was only 100 miles to Holland, we returned the rental late afternoon, and with plenty of daylight left, we headed for Holland. Somewhere in those miles, Dan called on the CB, said he had a rumbling noise, maybe the driveline. I asked if he could identify it and if not, we'd check it tomorrow cuz it'd be dark by the time we got to Holland. When we pulled into the motel, we knew it was going to be a good show, lots of kustoms already.

Friday morning we hurried to the fair-grounds. It was packed but had a nice cruise lane and grass parking. Friday went fast, we'd forgotten about the noise, I guess because we weren't cruising at 70mph...just low and slow. That night Dan reminded me – we'd better get it checked in the morning. We arrived at the fair-grounds early Saturday and got a great parking spot. We walked around checking out fantastic kustoms...the day whizzed past...again. Late afternoon, as everyone left, we decided to drive out to Holland State Park and shoot pics of the cars at sunset then find a restaurant. On the way out, Dan reminded me again about the noise in the rad '57.

"Too late now," I said. "Slipped my mind. Better check it tomorrow, see if I can recognize the noise." By that time, it was dusk, we decided to have a look around and got lost. We got so mixed up, we didn't know east from west in the flatlands of Michigan or which direction the sun had set - never did get to eat. We drove around aimlessly. When we saw headlights coming at us, we flagged the car down and asked where we were. He asked where we wanted to go and laughed, "Boys, you're ten miles from Holland" and gave us good directions. At the motel, the partying was going on and pals asked where we'd been...told them we got lost sightseeing...we got a ration about how did we get here from Denver then? The party went on until the wee hours and we slept in on Sunday...we made it to the fair-grounds about noon. Asked some locals where to get the '57 fixed. "Nothing open today, businesses are closed." Ooops. Guess we'll stay over.

Monday morning the weather didn't look good...cloudy and rain was forecast. Had to find a shop that could help us with what I figured was a relatively easy fix - bad rear wheel bearing. Called several places-all of them too busy to help us. OK, I'll do it myself! We finally found an auto parts store/machine shop as we were driving around. Stopped and asked if we could pull the rear wheels in their lot, check out the bearings and if bad, could they press new ones on? "Sure," the manager said, "need any tools or jack stands?" We had tools but we needed jack stands and an axle puller. Pulled driver's side first...bearing was fine. "It's the other side." Nope, it was good, too. We had a problem, not only with the driveline, but it started raining. With the car up on jackstands, I wondered about the rear-end since both bearings were good. I slipped back under it, dropped the driveshaft and grabbed the pinion with both hands and twisted. Nope, no move...put the tire iron cross wise and twist. Nope...there's our problem...and it's a big enough problem that it's never going to make 1000 miles home.

In the shop, Dan was drying off, asked if there were junk yards close to pull a '55-'64 third member, "only need 3:08's or a 3:36 geared pumpkin. If not a yard, can the machine shop rebuild ours?" They could, but it'd take a day to get parts from Detroit and a day to build it...the nearest junk yard was Grand Rapids, 30 miles away, but they were certain they didn't have anything older than 70's. "Anyone know some car guys around with extra parts?"

One of the guys in the machine shop overheard our predicament...said he had a '64 pumpkin at home but didn't know the ratio. The boss gave him time off to go get it and I crawled under the car to remove the third member...no choice now. Raining harder - streams of water ran under the car, soaking me – when you're a thousand miles from home ya gotta do whatever it takes to get a car back on the road. I've said it many times: IF you can't repair your car on the side of the road, you'd better leave it at home...or trailer it or stay at home! I can fix mine and have done so many times alongside the road.

The machine shop guy returned - 3:36 gears...perfect. Cleaned it, checked for bad teeth and made sure the pinion was free - pronounced it good enough for a long haul. We made a deal and I took it to the car...and the wet asphalt...at least, I could work under the car without rain on my eyeglasses, but it was coming down hard...typical Midwestern rainstorm...lightning crackling all around. Once bolted in, axles reinstalled, gear oil in and driveshaft mated, both Dan and I got soaked putting tires back on and getting the car off jackstands....at least it was warm rain, unlike ColoRODo's cold rain. I cleaned up, changed clothes, took the car for a test drive...no more rumbling – problem solved.

We thanked the manager, paid for the gaskets and gear oil but he wouldn't take money for the use of the jackstands. We left the shop at 2:00 PM...fastest major repair job on the side of the road I ever did. We drove well past Chicago before we stopped for the night and made it the rest of the way home the next day without further incident.

THE WAGON MOUND INCIDENT

Ya gotta go before you whoa! This story just proves not only us, but anyone can have road problems on a long distance trip.

October, 1993. Lake Havasu, Arizona. We'd had a good summer but Dan and I decided we should take in one more rod run, somewhere warm. It was starting to get chilly around Denver and the 16th Annual "Run to the Sun" was coming up. We'd been once before in our street rods and had a great time. This time we'd decided to take both '57 Chevys-the Mint Green radical chopped two-door hardtop and the full kustom gray 210 two-door. Dan would drive the hardtop and I would drive the gray car. We asked our friend Ed Banes and his wife Judy, if they'd want to go with us since they'd mentioned they'd like to go to Lake Havasu a couple of times. Ed had a really nice Teal colored '54 Chevy Sedan Delivery at the time with a 396" and a T-400 in it. Of course, the interior was gorgeous since that was ED's profession. We were good friends since Ed did all the interiors in all of our cars.

Las Vegas was to be our first stop on a two –day trip because snow south of Denver prevented us from going that way although the mountains west of Denver got snow as well, not as much as south of us. The Eisenhower tunnel and Vail Pass on I-70 were clear and passable. Once past Vail it would be clear sailing.

That first portion of our trip was uneventful, save for Ed having a minor problem with his starter. It would engage after quite a few tries but it always started after a gas stop. Ed commented he hoped it would last the trip. We arrived in Vegas late afternoon and hit the casinos right away, Judy always had great luck on the slots and this time was no different. Ed simply watched her play and after quite a few hours of playing, she cashed out and took 800 silver dollars out of the machine.

The next morning we weren't in a great hurry to get moving and it was a good thing. Ed's Delivery wouldn't start. He got out a

73

hammer and proceeded to whack the starter a few times, it worked and the car started. Ed said he'd had to do that a couple of times at home and he wasn't real worried about it but it was kind of embarrassing. It was already hot by the time we got out of Vegas so we decided not to go over the Hoover Dam and instead take Highway 95 through Searchlight and down to Needles, California to grab I-40. By the time we got to the California line it was already 100 degrees. Neither Dan or I had A/C in the '57's but Ed did and he told us he was "quite comfortable." Dan and I wanted warm, we didn't want extreme heat!

Lunch stop was in Needles-very hot Needles. The sky was bright blue and not a cloud in sight- should be a good weekend in Havasu. Crossing the Colorado River into Arizona, the 4th state we'd been in on this trip, there was only 8 miles to go before we turned off I-40 and headed south. Reaching the outskirts of Havasu in the late afternoon, we notice it's grown in the four years since we'd been there. A new airport, shopping malls and gas stations line the new four-lane highway. We knew we had a few miles to go to our motel when Dan called on the CB-said the brakes on the hardtop felt mushy. He had to pump like crazy to slow. I questioned him about it and he thought maybe a brake line had been severed somehow or a wheel cylinder was leaking bad. I told him to use the four-speed to slow himself and the e-brake if he had to stop quick. Figured we couldn't go too much farther into Havasu with all the traffic. Best thing to do is find a parts store. Fortunately a NAPA was just ahead so all three of us pulled into the lot.

Ed checked under the hood while Dan checked under the car. None of the tires had brake fluid showing on them so it wasn't wheel cylinders going bad. Rubber hoses on the front wheels were good, no leaks there. The master cylinder was empty, where'd all the fluid go? Ed suggested looking inside the car, under the dash where the push rod goes to the master cylinder. Sure enough, the insulation pad under the carpet was wet- the rubber boot had given out. Now what? Fix it, of course! NAPA didn't have a master cylinder for a '57 Chevy in stock-they could get one shipped in from Phoenix on Saturday. Nope!

That wouldn't work for us. How 'bout a rebuild kit? Yep, had one of those.

Back out to the parking lot and remove the lines and master cylinder. It's hot in Havasu, it's hot on the black asphalt parking lot, it's hot under the hood of the '57 but we'll live. Fortunately we are early to the rod run so we tell Ed to go find the motel we have reservations at and to instruct them Dan and I will be there later in the evening.

The master cylinder bore had some edges that need to be removed- we needed some Emory cloth and paper towels - back in to NAPA to buy more stuff. In the meantime, a few car guys see us in the parking lot and come over to offer help. I'd found some shade after I took the master cylinder off so worked on the bore. After sanding it, it was a lot smoother so reassembled it with new rubber boot and spring. Bolt it back on, fill it with fluid and bleed the brakes- not an easy task when the car sets only four inches above the ground. Yes, we had a jack and jack stands and raised the car to make it easier for me to get under it. Dan handled pumping the pedal and filling the fluid while I cracked the bleeder valves on the wheels. It took about three hours to take care of the problem and the sun had set but the job was done and we had good brakes again. No idea why the master cylinder decided to take a crap on the way, just thankful it wasn't in heavy traffic. Both Dan and I are hot and sweaty and smell bad, time to find the motel and take a shower.

Thursday morning, after checking in at the registration table, we found ourselves heading back to Nevada-the Riverside Casino in Laughlin was hosting the day's rod run. They had a special parking area for all the early arrivals and had coupons for play in the casino. We spent most of the day there playing the slots and watching the river boats ferry people to other casinos on the banks of the Colorado River and even across to Bullhead City in Arizona. Back in Havasu that evening, the "Relics & Rods" car club hosted their kick-off party at the Nautical Inn on the island. The show itself would start on Friday morning on the golf course. There were a lot of cars on the course when we rolled in and we knew there were many more coming in Friday night for the Saturday show. We had a great time checking out cars we'd never seen before and that's one reason we go to out-of-town rod runs, that, and seeing some great scenery in the United States.

Towards the end of Saturday, our radical '57 Chevy was picked for the "People's Choice" award. Sunday morning at 8 AM we got to drive through the awards ceremony in front of a huge crowd to receive the plaque. After the awards, about 11 AM, the show was over but there was a long parade on McCollough Boulevard to show-off most of the cars. Since we were going north, we just continued on out of Havasu up to I-40. We figured we could make it to Williams, Arizona for the night.

On Monday morning, Ed once again had trouble with the starter in his car so we didn't get an early start...as we drove east the sky started to appear dark. Just outside of Gallup, New Mexico, we drove into rain. That didn't last long but the pea-sized hail that followed did. It hailed so hard we had to slow because we couldn't see ten feet in front of us. It got to the point where the highway was covered and we couldn't even move, it was like driving on marbles, slipping and sliding all over the place. With no overpasses to hide under, we just pulled off the road and waited out the storm that lasted 30 minutes. Fortunately, the warm asphalt melted the hail reasonably quick so after the storm passed and the first few miles we were back up to speed, heading to our over-night in Albuquerque.

Tuesday morn, Ed's starter simply didn't want to work...it took about 15 minutes of whacking with the hammer to get the car started. Ed said he'd best not shut it off again or it won't start. From Albuquerque home it's a seven hour drive and about three tanks of gas. We drove through Las Vegas, New Mexico, through the southern part of the Sangre de Cristo mountains and the highway curved north onto the prairie headed towards the town of Raton and Raton Pass, the dividing line between New Mexico and Colorado. Ed called on the CB saying he can't make it to Raton, he needed fuel. The very small town of Wagon Mound is closest and it had only one gas station. We pulled in and Ed turned the car off. "Uh oh," he said. "Forgot, didn't want to do that. Hope it starts."

With the tank filled, Ed's car refused to start. Thirty minutes later, after nearly destroying the starter hammering on it, the battery is done. What now? Couple of options: Dan could drive back to Las Vegas to an auto parts store, get a new starter…forty-five miles there and forty-five back. Two hours round trip including finding a parts store or drive to Raton, 65 miles north, close to three hours round trip including finding a parts store. Ed said it's a waste of time and gas going back to Las Vegas, Raton would be easier since it's on the way home. He asked if we had a tow strap. Of course we do, we always do a long trip prepared. We hook the tow strap to the gray '57 and Roger heads out first, towing Ed north. Dan would follow behind the two cars. Slowly at first until Ed gets comfortable, then gain speed up to 70 mph.

Judy is scared stiff. She put her nose into a book and didn't look out the windshield one time on the way north. About halfway to Raton, a New Mexico Highway Patrolman going south gives us the eagle eye but he didn't make a U-turn so he must have decided it would be impossible to write a report on what he just saw. He kept going south. A little over an hour from Wagon Mound we pulled into Raton and found an auto parts store right away. Ed went in and comes back out with a starter, proceeds to jack up the car right there. Since it hadn't run for two hours, the engine was cold, made it easy to change the starter. When he took the old starter into the parts store, he found out he had the wrong starter in the car all this time. This starter was for a car engine, he had a truck starter in it. The car started easily and three hours later we were home to a cooler ColoRODo. The moral of this story is the same as all the past morals: If you can't fix it on the road, stay home…!!! Don't get to see much of the gorgeous scenery in the United States if you stay home..!!!

THE AMERICRUISE INCIDENT

At this point, you've read about our previous vacation incidents...have you noticed there are years that were skipped? Reason is – there were no vehicle problems on those "vacations" in those years. Fortunately, not all of our trips are "fix-it-on-the-side-of-the-road" mechanical issues...

June, 1994. Eastern Iowa. Dan and I heard about Tex Smith's "Teton Krooze" beginning in Driggs, Idaho, then connecting with the Americruise crew in Rapid City, then on to Peoria, Illinois. We thought it'd be fun so we mailed our registrations.

The second the postman picked it up, a friend - Lee Morrison, called..."Would you be our guests in Helper, Utah, at our Butch Cassidy Gang "Outlaw" show?" Hmmmmm, going to Utah would add miles from Denver and we'd have to leave a few days earlier - go west to end up east.

We took both '57 Chevys...me (Gray '57) and Dan (Mint Green chopped '57)...the Outlaw show pulled 80 cars on Friday/Saturday and we had a great time in the old mining town.

Head for Idaho on Sunday, through Salt Lake City to Hill AFB museum, north of SLC after that, two-lanes to Idaho.

Sunday night we arrived in Driggs ...Tex's "Krooze" would start Monday morn: through the Tetons, past Jackson; Riverton; up to Thermopolis; Worland; and over-night in Buffalo, Wyoming, 350 miles east of Driggs. We encountered "40 miles of bad road" (where are you, Duane Eddy?) on a cobbled under-construction two-lane road that was nerve-wracking in a car only four inches off the ground. Six miles wasted an hour but we got through it. The "Teton Krooze" ended in Rapid City, SD. However all during the Krooze, the 25 of us stayed together-we drove together. gassed up together, some times ate together, stayed at the same motel and seldom lost sight of each other on the highway. We finally met the Americruise bunch out of

Washington State...their ultimate destination, and ours: Peoria, Illinois, and "Three Sisters Park."

It wasn't Americruise, it was "Ameri-race." Wednesday morn driver's meeting: "Be at Dakota Digital in Sioux Falls by 5." Wasn't any "we'll drive 65, arrive together" or "cruise together, see the sights"...everyone was on their own – I was disappointed.

Dan and I drove easy...caught a rain storm close to Sioux Falls...so hard we stopped...eastern S.D. is flat...highway actually had two inches of standing water for miles...we poked along at 30, finally drove out of it.

We toured Dakota Digital and decided "home" was close - 150 miles south - the "cruisers" wouldn't miss us. That night, we stayed at Mom's, avoided a motel charge.

Thursday - typical Iowa overcast- gray, damp highways...driving by ourselves again, figured we'd catch the Americruisers in Calamus, Iowa, tour Yogi's Auto Parts. From our 'home' in Denison, we drove the 'Mother Road' -- Highway 30. Somewhere in the hills of eastern Iowa, fate awaited.

Running 60 mph up and down hills on that narrow two-lane, ditches waterlogged as Iowa had had rain for several days, we topped a hill, headed down. At the bottom, a mobile home towed by a pickup filled our lane, right turn signal blinking...safe enough, turning right onto a dirt road. Dan radioed he's going around and crossed the center-line. Just after he accelerated, the pickup also crossed the center-line. Uh-oh, they're turning left. Apparently their taillights were wired in reverse. There was no time for Dan to slow or stop, he was too close and I was directly behind - can't avoid an imminent collision. In my mind I see the rad '57 sideswiping the mobile home, then center-punching the pickup, possibly killing both drivers. I watched the '57's brake lights blink on, go out, then watched Dan's dual exhausts puff...he'd slammed the 4-speed into third, accelerated and slipped off the highway onto the muddy shoulder...mud flew as he rocketed past the mobile home/pickup. I'd lifted after seeing mud fly, but I was still going too fast - hoped the pickup driver was surprised by Dan flying past him...he was! The mobile home and truck was dead stopped in both lanes, I accelerated onto the shoulder, cleared the pickup just as an oncoming car neared.

My heart in my throat, scared as hell, ears pounding, knuckles bled white...waaaaay too close. Seemed like an hour later I finally breathed and heard the stereo. In reality, it'd been seconds but it all happened in slow motion. Dan's voice came over the CB, "Gotta stop, shaking so much I can't drive."

We pulled over...

My mind raced: we'd just escaped destruction. Our guardian angel rides with us, keeps us safe.

We made Peoria, Illinois, that afternoon...the "show 'n shine" would start Friday, at "Three Sisters" park, 15 miles northeast of Peoria.

Friday, we pulled into the "park"...only to be disappointed, again! The "park" was mowed corn/wheat fields...seems the 'three sisters' had left their land to the city, to be turned it into a park...except, it hadn't been 'turned' yet. The lane in was dirt and too many cars were attempting to get off the two-lane! Traffic jammed...the "staff" had everyone drive rows of a corn field, back and forth until the cars ahead of us got into the "park." Can you just picture the radical '57, which is only four inches off the ground plowing dirt and cornstalks in a just-cut cornfield? Unreal! The Three sister's house had been torn down, the area sprinkled with hay and vendors set up...it became a mud bog later.

All the "participants" were directed to the rear of the property, the wheat field had been mowed - our 'parking' for the day. I attempted to park on the lane that led to the rear of the property, didn't want to park in mud...once I was parallel parked between two cars, some guy yelled "Can't park there." Why not? He said, "Parking there is for the host club!" Not wanting to get into a fight, I moved. The wind started late afternoon, dust blew, shredded wheat stalks, corn stalks flew. Show n'shine be damned! Don't need my interior, or paint ruined. Dan and I left. On Saturday, after some area sight-seeing, we parked near the highway, wasn't about to park in fields. Sunday morn we left for Denver, didn't bother going back to "Three Sister's Park!. Needless to say, my Americruise incident was a bust.

I was so upset with "Three Sisters" park, I wrote a letter to the "title sponsor"... told them I'd never attend another Americruise...also wrote a letter to R & C magazine, told them how disappointed I was in their 'park" choice. Of course, I never got a return letter from either.

Sunday, as we headed home, we stopped in Ottumwa, Iowa, looking for Radar O'Reilly - wasn't listed in the phone book and couldn't find his farm. A few miles out of town we saw a sign: "Air Museum-next left." Sounded good but it was late, we over-nighted in Ottumwa. Next morning we took the county road to the museum, but a glint of sun off automobile glass hidden in the tree line on the right side of the road stopped us. Not one, but fifty-sixty autos lined a fence...gotta stop! We asked the owner if we could 'look.' "Sure, there's cows and goats in there, oh, might be some Bull snakes, too." Lots of fifties and sixties cars...in one of the ravines '60's cars were piled on top of '50's cars, on top of '40's cars and under thoughse,'30's...it'd take a massive effort to salvage them and there were hundreds of cars in several ravines. Spent four hours there, then drove to the air museum. Two guys came out of the hangars as we pulled in, one the owner - gave us a personal guided tour...there were historic Bi-planes, early Iowa aviation memorabilia, some WWI and WWII stuff - Americana is alive and well off the Interstates and it looks better through the windshield of a hot rod or a kustom. After spending several hours there, we continued across southern Iowa, home was 700 miles away.

THE OHIO INCIDENT

Having never been 'deep south' on a rod run, the town of Pigeon Forge, Tennessee, was a giant tourist mecca and the farthest we've been south. This incident happened while we were in the second week of a two week vacation and had driven north to Ohio.

July, 1995. Xenia, Ohio. Dan and I usually decide where we want to go for the summer, in January, meaning - which rod run in which part of the country.

We made plans to attend the Pigeon Forge, Tennessee, KOA event, and to take only one car... the radical '57. Figured the rad '57 could make the trip - everything in it was new. It felt strange having my brother riding in the same car since we were used to taking two cars to every event we went to.

It took three days from Denver and we enjoyed the trip – Pigeon Forge is a tourist mecca, Gatlinburg was unreal and crowded, the Smokies were bigger than I'd imagined and there were lots of Civil War places to see...the KOA show and a week went fast. During the event, we'd heard about the "Fiesta of the 50's" event in Xenia, Ohio, the next weekend and since we were in no hurry to get back to Denver we thought we'd hang around the area, do some sight-seeing and eventually make to way to Ohio. Best part is Xenia wasn't that far from Dayton...and Dayton had one of the sights we'd always wanted to tour...to be more precise – the Wright Patterson AFB's huge Unightd States Air Force museum.

We decided to take the whole week and play tourist. On Monday, we headed east and north from Pigeon Forge. We visited sites in North Carolina (Cherokee and the Great Smoky Mountains), parts of Virginia (Cumberland Gap and Civil War monuments) and Kentucky (the Corvette Assembly plant in Bowling Green), and Mammoth Caves, we planned on spending a day there. Once there, we parked the '57 in the fringes of the heavily treed parking lot so no one could park next to us, tossed the car cover over it and locked it under the car…out of sight, out of mind, ya know? The cave tour took several hours ending late afternoon. We decided to stay over-night close by…as we headed for our car we saw a young guy walking around it, looking, but not touching or lifting the car cover. What's he doing? We hung back and waited to see what he was up to. Finally, he ambled off and we didn't pay much attention which direction he went as long as it was away. As we were uncovering the car, he came running back.

"I knew it," he yelled, "I just knew it was that car."

"What do you mean?" I asked, not exactly sure what he was talking about.

"This car," he said, pulling a magazine out of his back pocket. "I knew it had to be. The paint color showing under the edges of the car cover…and how low it is." He opened the mag. Yep, there it was: our radical '57 in Rod & Custom magazine, (June, 1994 issue). "Will you guys autograph this for me?"

"Serious?" we asked. He handed us a pen and the mag.

"You're from ColoRODo, right? It amazes me to see this car here. I didn't think I'd ever see a famous magazine car in Kentucky."

We explained it wasn't a famous magazine car, it was built as a driver and that's what we were doing…he wasn't accepting any of it. He wanted to know all about our trip and shot photos of us next to the car. Funny thing is, I don't ever remember getting his name. We chatted as we put our car cover away, finally said our goodbyes and drove off to find a motel.

The next day -Wednesday, we'd been using A/C most of the time cuz it's humid back east and us ColoRODoans are not used to that. Somewhere in Ohio, nearing our final destination, we pulled into a gas station in a small town. Dan pumped fuel while I checked under the hood…I'd been hearing a strange clicking noise for the last few miles, and I always keep track of the gauges cuz I don't like engine surprises on a long trip (who does?). I put my hand on the A/C compressor to check the oil and I almost fell into the engine compartment. The A/C compressor simply fell off the bracket. It missed putting a big dent in the radiator by half an inch. I unhooked the belt, lifted it out of the engine compartment and set it on the ground.

"What the hell?" Dan asked from behind the car. "Why'd you do that?"

"Bracket broke," I said, showing him the ragged edge, "We were less than a mile from a major radiator problem. Would have bent the fan, destroyed the radiator and maybe the battery if it bounced around and I didn't get stopped fast enough," I said, pulling the belt off the pulley to put both in the trunk. "Guess we're going to have to rely on 4-70 A/C from now on...looks like my welding skill needs improvement!" That incident would have cost us more than two or three days in Small Town, Ohio - patching an aluminum radiator or finding parts we'd need to repair the damage...luckily, we didn't have to.

We arrived in Xenia on Thursday afternoon, found our motel and since the event didn't start til Saturday, had a day to kill...early Friday morn we hightailed it to the air museum in Dayton. Spent the entire day there...and didn't see it all...figured we'd have more time after the event.

The Xenia event was fun...got to see lots of cars we never see anywhere else...cars that wouldn't make long trips like we just did...most participants couldn't believe we'd driven the very low, very chopped rad '57 all the way from ColoRODo (and FYI, it didn't have air bags!).

Saturday night we talked about Dayton again - Sunday mornings at rod runs are rather slow and sparse - we loaded the car at 7 AM, checked out of the motel and headed for the air museum. Several rod run participants passed us coming in as we were driving out of Xenia...they waved, we waved.

We finished the museum about 1:00 that afternoon and headed back to Xenia...as we pulled into the grounds where the event was held, we were met with "Glad you guys are back," and "Saw you leaving, figured you were headed home," and "Didn't expect you back." We explained we had to "finish" our museum tour. Later that afternoon, we found out why everyone was so concerned about our late Sunday arrival...we'd won "People's Choice" and of course, the

"Long Distance" award…to say that the promoter was terribly upset that we'd 'gone home' in the morning without telling anyone would be an understatement. He was very relieved when we showed up cuz he (told us he) didn't want to give the award to someone else.

The People's Choice award was a "Big Boy" (Restaurant) six foot trophy which we had to take apart to put in the back seat. About 4 that afternoon, after photos were shot and handshakes all around, we said our goodbyes and headed for parts west…we still had 5 hours of Midwest daylight left for driving.

THE DIAMOND INCIDENT

Diamonds in a drawstring black pouch? Yep! How many? Lots of them! We just didn't know how to value the full bag of them.

June, 1996. Dayton, Ohio. Dan and I decided to take the chopped radical '57 Chevy on another solo trip riding together, this time to Good-guys Indianapolis event and then Richmond, Indiana for the KOA Double Date event. We went with friends –Hal Nelson ('53 Cadillac with a 500" V8), Kirk Severson (and wife), black '32 Ford roadster with blown 350", and my son, Chris, and friend Dave, in his '65 Chevy flat window van, with a very large 350" V8 inside.

We left Denver at 7AM on a bright sunny ColoRODo day…once we got into Kansas, it got hotter… humidity, ugh! Kirk decided the black top on his black roadster w/black interior was too hot, so he pulled into a rest stop to remove the top, in the shade…!!! The thermometer on the vend building read 100 degrees…I wondered what the sun was going to do to Kirk and his wife on the open highway…even with my windows down, the breeze felt blast furnace hot.

Easy Jack's junk yard was our first stop just outside Junction City, Kansas. We'd never been but heard about it. After walking around for several hours (yes, the yard was THAT big), we decided we'd better put some miles on…down the on-ramp we flew…until Hal nailed the Caddy to gain some "merge" speed and immediately slowed.

"Car no move," he said over the CB, "maybe u-joints just left."

"Tranny die?" Kirk responded. We stopped, see if we could get him going. He got out of the car, opened the hood to see if anything was amiss and then said "I'd better get out my tool box, it's under the seat."

We waited in front of that very hot engine compartment for him to bring his tool box, until we realized that no tool box would fit under the seat of a Caddy. Peering around the hood, he's on the phone, talking to his mechanic in Denver. He hung up, minutes later phone rings, his mechanic has called Junction City- a tow truck is coming.

Time drags as we wait. The truck showed up, loaded up and asked where to deliver -to a tranny shop in Junction City, we follow as the truck pulled into the driveway of an old looking tranny shop, a grizzled old man in greasy coveralls bolts out the bay door, "Don't drop that thing here, I ain't working on it."

"It's 5:30," Hal yelled, "where else can I take it?"

By the time the old man and Hal were done talking, the Caddy was on the hoist and everyone was under it trying to figure out what's broken.

While Hal, Kirk and the old man examined, the rest of us were hungry. The trip was on hold – so food and a motel next.

During the night, the Midwest Monsoon arrived...rain like I ain't never seen...no driving in that, besides, it rained so hard, the Interstate was closed in portions.

Meanwhile, back at the tranny shop- the main input shaft had twisted off the 700R-4, had to be ordered out of Topeka, arrival about noon - an all-day fix. Mid-afternoon, the rain eased and we were told - "Don't wait any longer for us. Go!" Dan, I, Chris and his pal said okay and headed east...see ya in Indy.

We drove on damp highways until well past Kansas City...near St. Louis it finally dried, over-nighted in Vandalia.

The next day we were in Indy. Off the Interstate, on some side streets we found a line of hot rods about two miles long...the registration line? We got in line and waited...and waited...and waited...no movement. I walked to the front, found out everyone was waiting to get into the Indy 500 track for a lap or two. I asked where the hotel/registration was and left. At the hotel we found out Hal got his Caddy fixed and Kirk and his wife had first or second degree sunburns.

GG's Indy was a blast, especially with nostalgic drag racing going on at the same time, but it was a real mud pit after it rained, and it did in the afternoon. Never could figure out why anyone, with a nice clean car (and undercarriage) would leave a facility, drive to wherever in a rain storm and get the car totally dirty instead of waiting for rain to stop…!!! Besides, the Indy event had one way in…and the same way out…what a mad, muddy rush for the 'door'…we waited until late afternoon when the rain, and the rush was finished.

Monday morn we headed for parts unknown. Chris and his friend decided to head for Cleveland, Ohio, and all the giant roller coasters. We were to meet friends Ken & Debby Carpenter in Dayton, tour Butch's Rod Shop, then spend the night at the Carpenter's place in Fairfield, Ohio.

Before that happened, we gassed up in a Dayton suburb. While under the hood checking oil and water, a new Cadillac pulled in, guy in a suit gets out, reaches for the gas pump and fills his Caddy. He glanced over at the radical '57, then walked around it. Didn't think much of it as many people like to look at the rad '57…ask if we "drove it all the way from ColoRODo." The well-dressed man looked at the engine and interior of our '57 and asked about it. I explained what it was and saw him glance at the small "For Sale" sign in the front window. "Is it really for sale?"

"It is," I answered.

"How much," he asked.

"Thirty-five," I said calmly, having been asked that question a million times ever since we got the car done and each time we'd get the same answer –"Oh!"

"I'd like to own that car," he said. "But I don't have that much?"

Was I shocked? No, not really…I'd heard it before.

"I could give you that much cash, but then I wouldn't have any for the rest of the week," he said, adjusting his expensive tie. "Would you be willing to take two thousand cash and the rest in diamonds?"

I was taken aback by the offer.

"You want to give me two thousand in cash and the rest in diamonds," I stammered, trying to comprehend how I'm going to figure out how much diamonds are really worth…and how big a bag full I'd get.

"Yes, but it might take a few hours to put together that much in diamonds. I'd have to go to my store. Would you wait for me to do that?"

"Hold on, help me understand this," I said. "You're going to give me two thousand dollars, in cash, and you want me to accept 33 thousand dollars worth of diamonds. How will I know they're worth what you say they are?"

The look on his face was priceless...he's taken aback! With a stunned voice he said, "You want thirty-five thousand dollars, not thirty-five hundred?"

"Yes," I said, not really surprised he misinterpreted my price.

He didn't say another word...got into his Cadillac and drove off. Dan and I got into the '57, laughing about our failed 'near deal' as we headed out.

To this day, we still get a chuckle out of the diamond dealer that thought he was going to buy a finished, award winning toy...really cheap. It's a great story, worth telling over and over.

THE "MY CLASSIC CAR" INCIDENT

Our very FIRST fifteen minutes of fame...and we're still enjoying it to this day!

June, 1996. Richmond, Ohio. For the second leg of our two week trip, this after spending the weekend in Indy at the Good-guys event (and the previous 'Indy/Diamond Incident'), the plan was to continue to our ultimate destination, Richmond, Indiana, for the Second Annual KOA "Double Date" event...but first, on Monday, we said our goodbyes to my son Chris and his friend Dave. They had decided to go to Cedar Point Amusement Park in Cleveland, Ohio to ride the roller coasters. We told them to meet us in Richmond at week's end so we could travel back to Denver together on Monday. So, with that taken care of, Dan and I called my new friend, Kevin Anderson, owner of Anderson Advertising in Indianapolis and drove over to his agency digs. After looking over his chopped '50 Merc and chatting in his studio for over an hour, it was time for lunch. He invited us to one of his favorite restaurants in a small town called Zionsville. It was a nice low-key country-style restaurant and the food was delicious. After we were fully fed and the conversation drifted around to "Which way are you going to Richmond? There's some interesting attractions on the way you might want to see." We said "Yep, sight-seeing is our middle name," and then a "We'll see ya in Richmond," said goodbye to Kevin and we took some two-lane back roads on the way. We found quite a few of those attractions along the way, took our time and stayed over-night in a small, nameless Indiana burg.

Our friends, Ken and Debby Carpenter were expecting us Tuesday afternoon, we were to meet them at Butch's Rod Shop Tuesday and from there follow them to their home in Fairfield. Once at Ken & Debby's home, we got to check out Ken's garage and his '50 Merc and his '37 DeSoto coop he was working on, after, we had a great BBQ that evening on Ken and Debby's patio.

Since we had a few days to "kill" before the KOA event and Dan and I love to ride roller coasters… Ken and Debbie insisted we take their late model Cadillac (and leave the radical '57 Chevy in the garage behind their house) on Wednesday morning and drive up to King's Island amusement park and ride all the roller coasters the park had. We got back to the Carpenter's home late, mainly cuz we were having such a great time, we hurried off to a small cruise-in at a drive-in somewhere in Fairfield, checked out some local cars and ate our fill of chili cheese hot dogs.

On Thursday morn, we drove to Richmond…Dan got to drive Ken's '50 Mercury up and we followed Debbie through Oxford, home of the Miami University…there were lots of interesting old architecture around there and we enjoyed the side trip. The KOA event officially started on Friday, so we helped Ken and Debbie get the fair-grounds all set up in the afternoon and then we checked into our motel for the weekend.

Friday morning, we learned that Dennis Gage and his "My Classic Car" film crew had been invited to attend the show in hopes they'd shoot some of it for airing…seeing as how his show was new, covering this event would be their 4th episode…if they showed up.

My son, Chris, and his friend Dave, finally showed up in Richmond on Friday regaling us tales of bigger, higher and faster roller coasters than we had been on…they spent two days at the Cedar Point Amusement Park in Sandusky …they also regaled us with tales of their visit to the Cleveland Rock 'n Roll Hall of Fame.

Friday night, at the event, a flamethrower contest was held…and so was a neon light parade…we didn't participate in either cuz we don't have flamethrowers on the '57's…and the neon green stick I'd had in the grille broke on the trip there.

Saturday morn the weather was hot and humid…lots of cars showed up and it looked like it was to be a great show. Dan and I always walk around to check out every car there (what's the sense of driving to a far-away car event to sit on your as…uhm…lawn chair, behind your car and not look at any other cars or even talk to other people…???). IMHO, if you drive a long distance and then just sit in a lawn chair, you'd just as well stay home, watch rust form, paint dry or grass grow. Anyway, we saw Dennis Gage and his handle-bar mustache checking out a few of the cars and filming them...we watched for a while as he interviewed the owners...it was kinda cool to see how they did it for TV – there wasn't any real TV magic there. While Dennis was being Dennis, we continued to walk around the grounds checking out kool kustoms until we heard someone yelling our names...it was my friend, Kevin Anderson, the guy responsible for getting Dennis Gage there (he'd promised him a ride around the grounds in his chopped '50 Merc and said he could film part of the show that way), he told us we needed to get back to our '57 right away as Dennis had fallen in love with it and he wanted to interview us and film the car.

We walked back to the car, met Dennis and shook hands with him...he asked us if we could move the car to a better location for filming and we obliged...all the while he was filming and interviewing us, he kept saying, "I absolutely love this car...when I get rich and famous, I'm going to buy it from you." (Strangest thing is, that was a lot of years ago, he's never contacted me to buy it after his TV show became popular). Sad to say, I was hoping someone famous would buy it...but nooo-ooo-oooo!

I think they shot an hour's worth of film on the car and boiled it all down to about a five minute segment in the coverage of the "Double Date" on the "My Classic Car" show. The best part of that filming is about a month later they sent us a complete video of the show...and for several years after it first aired on TV, we'd have people come up to us at a rod run somewhere and tell us they "saw your '57 on TV last night." I really don't know how many times that particular episode was aired, I lost count after ten reruns, but I'd bet it was a lot more than any other.

Dennis Gage and "My Classic Car" had us sign a "guest appearance" release form, paid us for being on their "TV Show" (a nice crisp new one dollar bill) and gave us a "My Classic Car" T-shirt for being in their video...the T-shirt and dollar bill were framed and they're still hanging on the wall...just another 15 minutes of "our" fame...!!!

THE DEER INCIDENT

They say accidents occur within 35 miles of home...well, "they" are correct. This incident occurred about 24 miles from home. We'd been driving all day and wanted to get home to our own beds that particular night. We usually don't drive when it gets dark and usually find a motel about 5:30 or 6 in the afternoon, but since we were so close to home, and knew the roads and how people in the area drove, we chanced it. Shouldn't have!

November, 1999. Franktown, ColoRODo. We'd left Scottsdale, AZ, and the Good-guys event Sunday after the awards. My brother, Dan was driving my Gray'57, I'm driving the chopped '57 Chevy hardtop. We drove to Gallup, New Mexico. The weather'd been decent and there'd been no snow at that point. In the motel, map in front of us, we decided to run two-lanes to Farmington, NM. Since I hate Interstates, the "back way," through the San Juan Mountains, would be scenic. We took Highway 64 from Farmington to Chama, then headed northeast for Cumbres Pass (elevation 10,022 feet), the same pass the Cumbres and Toltec scenic railroad runs over...the plan was to get to Alamosa and then grab I-25 at Walsenburg, home would be three hours away from there.

We didn't realize there'd be a lot of snow already on the southern ColoRODo passes in November. Cumbres Pass was scary as we 'dropped' into the valley, then over La Manga Pass (10,230 feet). Took us 3 hours to travel 47 miles and slipped, literally, into the town of Antonito, ColoRODo. Since our cars were running street tires...sliding down curvy mountain roads at 10 mph was not exactly fun and quite nerve wracking. Needless to say, we'd questioned our decision many times going over those two passes.

Anyway, we shot through Walsenburg and by the time we got to Pueblo, it was dark-thirty and we had 120 miles to go for home, but we'd sleep in our own beds. We'd gassed up in Pueblo, grabbed a McD's and hit the Interstate, looking forward to getting through ColoRODo Springs, cause we'd grab a little-traveled two-lane just north of there…we call it the 'back way,' goes through Black Forest and there's no traffic…besides, the Interstate between the Springs and Denver is a 60 mile long NASCAR race…people are nuts, drive about 95 mph and it's always "get-the-hell-out-of-my-way-cuz-I'm-comin'-through!"

The two-lane was dry, but at 8:30 PM, quite cold as a snowstorm had gone through a few days prior, there was snow piled alongside the highway…ugh, more snow!

I was leading in the rad hardtop, don't know why cuz I usually follow Dan since he knows where he's going all the time and I don't have to watch traffic- he's cutting the path. I was anxious to get home…it'd been a long day and we were tired.

Approaching Franktown - nothing more than an intersection 17 miles from home, the highway drops off the high plateau and curves its way down the face, probably runs downhill for two miles - it's the most curvy part of the road. The speed limit is 45 through there, Dan is about five car lengths behind me and I'm coasting - meaning foot off the accelerator. I see headlights coming up the hill and make sure I'm in my lane…the exact second the headlights get alongside me, I heard a loud craaa-aaack. You have to know it was loud since I always have the stereo cranking out the tuneage…I thought to myself, what did that guy do, drop off the edge of the pavement and hit the road's edge steel barriers? The taillights passed me and I let the thought pass, too. The CB crackled to life, Dan's yelling, "Rog, I just hit a deer. I've gotta stop," his voice breaking up, definitely scared but hopefully not hurt physically.

"You OK?" I asked, immediately stopping in the lane and finding reverse gear.

"I think so, but I wrecked your car," he yelled, certainly shook up.

"Relax, relax a bit. As long as you're OK, it's OK. Find the flashlight, see what kind of damage there is…I'm backing up." There was no traffic as I backed up the hill…Dan is out surveying the car when I stop. I see taillights in the other lane, up the hill, a block or so behind us…appears to be stopped, too.

"It looks bad," Dan said, hands shaking. "I'm sorry. I really wrecked your car…and the engine just quit after I hit it."

"See if you can open the hood," I said, shining the flashlight behind the car to see the deer carcass all torn to shreds. "Let's see if the radiator is hurt. I don't see any anti-freeze running, just blood and guts all over."

Just about that time, a voice comes out of the darkness "Did you guys hit that deer too?" A woman, about 35 or so, walks into our little circle of light. "I hit it first. My truck is totaled, I've called my husband, he's on the way. I'm about to call the highway Patrol, do you want to report the accident?"

"Are you OK…??? I asked. "You must have been the headlights that just passed me." She said the deer had come out of the ditch just as she passed me…she couldn't avoid it and knocked it into Dan's lane…Dan literally ran over the carcass…and with the custom-built air dam below the bumper on the gray '57, only four inches above the asphalt, the '57 literally tore the animal apart as Dan bounced over it.

We checked the '57 over…the air dam was folded under the bumper, the bumper was skewed…looked like Dan nailed the deer dead center of the car. The fenders, prone to buckling easily on a '57 were not damaged, nor was the hood. I attributed that to me building in "overkill" on the air dam. I'd built the air dam with ¼" round rod and reinforced the bumper brackets, it was 'solid'…figured if something got hit with the air dam, it'd not take much damage. I was correct. After our short inspection, I told Dan to try to start it. Surprisingly, it fired up…the exhausts were really loud…probably tore off the pipes or headers busted up bad. We checked the radiator again – no leaks, good to go. I felt around, one header was ripped at the flanges and the other side damaged and leaking.

We asked the woman again if she was OK, she said just shook up. I told her our car wasn't badly damaged - nothing I couldn't fix. We headed home, Dan and I both thanking our guardian angel one more time for watching over us on our trips and very thankful the lady's truck hit the deer first. If she hadn't, we'd still be rebuilding the entire front end on the radical '57. We got home about 11:30 PM and put the cars in the garage…not much to do about the damage til morning.

The next morn I opened the garage door and whoa, talk about stink…nearly knocked me down! I left the door open for a while and jacked up the '57 to view the damage. Blood, guts and deer hair/flesh covered the undercarriage. When Dan came over he recounted the scene – "I saw the deer come across in front of me in a flash, but I thought it was upright when I hit it, but it may not have been. I felt the car bounce up over it. With the '57 so low, the headers helped tear it apart."

He felt bad about wrecking my car, but it's something that can/will happen when you drive your car. I told him again, like I did that night, "Don't worry about it. It happens. Metal can be fixed…people not so much." Since it was late November and we weren't doing more trips, we'd repair the car by spring and no one would even know the car was in an accident…it got done. Two years later, I sold the Gray '57 Chevy and the Chopped Mint Green radical kustom '57 Bel Air hardtop was sold in 2015.

THE KANSAS INCIDENT

Fortunately, there were no "incidents" in the four years between these two stories even though we went rod running every summer. In 1999, Roger "retired" from a formal 8-5 job so there was no need to ask for vacation days or time off, we just decided where we wanted to go and when and got the cars ready and took off.

August, 2000. Mid-Kansas. So there we were winging it across hot Kansas...Dan was driving the gray '57, I'm cruising the radical '57...we're headed for the Gas Capital rod run in Hugoton, Kansas... on two lane highways, of course. We'd never been to this rod run before, but we'd gotten a personal invitation from Ralph Rodgers after I'd inquired about the event. Ralph told me they were giving away a 'few' cash prizes and cash always gets my attention...!!!

Hugoton is about 300 miles southeast of Denver... a mere hop and a skip for Dan and I - a little over a four hour drive, normally...we left late Thursday morn intending to roll in late afternoon, wash the cars and relax a bit before Friday morning's festivities started.

We were running Highway 50 and once we'd crossed into Kansas, it got hotter than blue blazes, the humidity was killing us cuz neither of us had A/C in our cars. We headed east, toward Garden City, we've got plenty of 4-70 air (4 windows down at 70 miles per), but that was akin to standing next to a blast furnace and I could only imagine the black asphalt highway surface was at least 940 degrees. I think that's what led to the near tragedy when the left rear BFG tire on the gray '57 started coming apart...peeling off...literally shedding tread. Dan didn't even have time to call on the CB. I was following him, the tire coming apart under the car, banging the fenderwell and flying toward me...not only was it coming apart, but he was sliding around both lanes of the highway like a Top Fuel car on ball bearings, trying to hold on to the car as the tire sheds chunks. I'm yelling at him, "Don't let it get away," even though I didn't have the CB in my hand. I'm sure he was cussing at the same time…!!! After taking up both lanes more than once, he finally got the car stopped just off the shoulder. The only thing holding the air in the tires was the steel belts…not much left of the carcass…the tread was gone, it looked like a semi-bald cartoon character with wire hanging out all over for hair.

"How'd that happen?" I asked as Dan got out of the car, shaking, "You hit something?"

"Didn't think I was going to keep it on the highway," he said, motioning to the 15-20 foot deep ditch that ran alongside the highway. "Good thing no one was coming toward me while I was fighting that. Hey, wasn't that a new tire?"

"It is…was…it was a new BF Goodrich last week," I said. "It sure came apart."

"Looks like our guardian angel still rides with us," Dan said.

"Yeah, that could have ended up a lot worse." I started to get the jack out of the trunk and loosen the lug nuts on the wide tire on my gray '57. I knew it wasn't going to be easy to change since it's so wide on this Chevy, we had to jack the car up, slip a jackstand (yep, always carry one with us) under the frame and remove the shock, that effectively lowered the axle and gave us enough room to fight the wide tire out from under the car. The tire carcass was hot, I was sweating, the steel was jagged and trying to hold onto the way hot rim wasn't exactly the easiest thing to do. Some of the steel belts had wrapped around the axle as it rolled and were trying to strangle the brake line – great, just what we need! Dan got out the wire cutters and I started trimming. The worst part was trying to get the tire off without gloves - my hands bled, but it got done. The spare looked mighty strange…and skinny, once we got it under the car.

"That ain't going to work," I said, as we let it down off the jack. I stood back and looked at the rear of the car - one skinny tire and one wide tire made the car look lopsided. Once we got underway I took the back door, following Dan, eyeballing the skinny tire under the two door '57. "That skinny tire is ugly!"

"Well, we can head into Garden City and find a tire store, see if they've got a wider one, but it's about 22 miles farther east…we were going to take Highway 25 south at Lakin just ahead," Dan radioed, "Small town."

"It's a cinch we're not going to find a wide tire in Lakin…has to be a larger town, like Garden City. Yeah, let's do that…that '57 can't go to Hugoton with an ugly black rim and uglier spare tire on the car," I said.

It took seven different tire stores in Garden City before we found a tire that would match the size and width…and 2 ½ hours. At that point, it looked like we weren't going to get to Hugoton til after dark.

Once we had the tire mounted on the American Racing Daisy five spoke, we headed south on Highway 83, down to Highway 56 and then back west…the highways were dwarfed by the many cornfields. Right at dusk it must've been time for the yellow moths to start leaving the cornfields cuz we ran into them…thousands of them…they changed the front of the gray car and grille to yellow and the windshield to mush. The Mint Green radical '57 looked like someone had topped the ice cream with sprinkles and the chopped windshield was covered in squashed bodies and very hard to see out of.

We arrived safely and found the motel…it was late so we'd wash the cars in the morning.

Well, the Gas Capital Rod Run was a huge success, it was held in the city park and about 120 cars showed up…a BBQ was held that night and on Sunday the awards were handed out…the Jetter Brothers took home several awards: our Mint Green Radical kustom '57 Chevy won a plaque for "Best Body," sponsored by Bob's Auto Body, and a check for $100.00. Dan and the gray '57 won 2nd place "Long Distance" - a plaque and $50.00, I won third "Long Distance" – a plaque and $25.00…and the capper for the weekend was the radical '57 won "Participant's Choice" - a plaque and a check for $100.00… tire money (and gas money)! I've never been to a rod run anywhere that gave out that much money as awards…and…I haven't since. However, I must add, our '57's weren't the only cars that won cash…Kudos to Ralph Rodgers, the trophy sponsors and the Hugoton bunch.

After the awards, we headed south for Liberal cuz we'd seen signs along the way for a great air museum there...we spent the night in Liberal and the temps, and humidity never did cool off. We were at the museum when it opened the next morn, spent a couple of hours there and then took some county roads heading north and west...once past Lamar, ColoRODo, we could feel the humidity going away as we got closer to Denver...we got home Monday night without a problem.

HALF WAY!

Well, you're about half way through this book and I'm wondering what you're thinking about the stories herein...??? Maybe you're thinking: *these guys have more-on-the-road troubles than anyone I'd ever heard of!* OR: *Wow! They can't build a car worth a damn!* OR: *I'd bet half of these stories are not true and simply made up.* OR: *This book is nothing more than bragging about how well their cars are built.*

You'd be partially correct on the last statement. Over the years Dan and I have built, driven and sold several cars. By "build" I mean frame-off, new engines, new suspension, new wiring, new interiors, new glass, new paint and anything and everything that accompanies 'building' a car from an assorted pile of junk parts.

But in reality, this book is simply to point out that ANYTHING mechanical is prone to fail at any point in its life, whether it's down the street from your home or on an 1800 mile trip and whether it's in a street rod or a kustom, a classic or a stocker! You'll read in here that just because a part is new doesn't necessarily make it work as intended and you can thank the companies that choose to buy their parts from the Chinese for that. New does not mean new these days! The next to last story in this book is a perfect example of brand new stuff purchased from NAPA that didn't work- it lasted maybe a week before it finally took a crap.

Not only are these stories about parts failures, but they are about taking your rebuilt car out on the highway of this great country and seeing the sights. If you've built your car to your own exacting specifications and didn't cut corners, then you shouldn't be afraid to take a 1000 mile (or more) trip in it. The stories herein are about how a car can be fixed on the side of the road and IF you've built your car, you know exactly how everything in it works and how to fix it without needing a professional in the next city! Of course, there are some parts of the car that cannot be fixed on the side of the road - transmissions being the worst. Thankfully, Dan and I have never experienced a failed transmission but we have nearly everything else!

Over the four decades Dan and I have been rod running across this country (and Canada) we have literally put over a million cumulative miles on our various cars. To say we have complete confidence in our builds might be an understatement but we are not afraid to jump in our cars and go somewhere, anywhere, any time!

Roger and Dan

THE TEXAS INCIDENT

*This incident occurred when we'd decided to go to a Kustom
Kemps Of America event in Denison, Texas...the first KKOA show
we'd been to since 1992.*

October, 2000. Denison, Texas. Dan and I decided to go to
Texas for a late fall outdoor kustom car show in Denison. No, not our
hometown, ours was in Iowa. We met up with Dave Pareso and his
GF, Chris, driving their chopped orange/flamed '51 Mercury, Shane
Savage and his chopped '48 "High School Confidential" Chevy coop
and a couple of other guys from the 'Springs' with their kustoms mid-
morning. I was driving the radical '57 Chevy hardtop and Dan cruised
the gray '57 two door.
 As Dan followed me down to the 'Springs to meet up with Dave, he
told me I was blowing a lot of dark smoke out of the right bank
exhaust, especially when I accelerated or let off the gas too slow. "We
can check it out when we get to Dave's Place," he said. Everyone was
ready when we arrived...checking the oil got spaced out and we all
hit the road. We ran Highway 50 east across ColoRODo and our first
gas stop was in Lamar, 78 miles north of the ColoRODo/Oklahoma
state line. I checked the oil as Dan filled both cars with gas. The oil
was a little low on the dipstick, but it was good to go. Figured we'd
check it again at the next gas stop.
    Back on the road we had to stop at the state line of Oklahoma as
the engine developed a miss. We checked the plugs on the right head
and found one was fouled a bit, we cleaned it up and put it back in.
We drove into Boise City, Oklahoma, around the courthouse square
and east out of town, then south and crossed into Texas. Oklahoma on
Highway 287 (Oklahoma Highway 385) is only 45 miles wide so it
doesn't take long to get into and out of the state. We were making
good time and the area was flat and not real hot at this time in mid-
October so the gas mileage was good. Dumas, Texas, was our next
stop for gas and it was starting to get dark. We pulled into a station

and filled up. I again checked the oil, it was near two quarts low. While filling the tank, I'd noticed there was dark exhaust residue building up on the trunk deck above the right exhaust tip. That wasn't looking good- the engine used a lot of oil to cover three hundred miles. May have a serious problem here. As long as the oil consumption doesn't get worse, we should be OK. I added oil and figured I'd check it again when we got to Amarillo for the night.

The next morning before firing up the car I checked the oil. It was down on the dipstick. Not good. I looked for a leak around the valve cover gaskets and checked the drain plug on the oil pan to make sure it was tight. Everything looked okay, so I checked the plugs and wires thinking one of the cylinders wasn't firing, causing the use of oil. The wire on the No. 8 cylinder was brittle, it had been touching the header so we decided to change it. Hmmmm, maybe that's part of the problem. Dan carried a couple of extra plug wires in his trunk thinking maybe we'd need them some day, now's the time. I pulled the plug out of No.8 cylinder just to check it and it was covered in black oil, like it wasn't burning at all - rings may have gone bad on this cylinder, the engine does have lots of miles on it. Dave said we should try some hotter plugs and he whipped out a package he had stashed in his trunk and gave us one. They were hotter than what we were running and I stuck it back into the hole, connected the new wire and put two quarts of oil in. We were ready for the road, hopefully a hotter plug would not foul like this one did, hoping that perhaps the rings were not damaged on the piston.

Our next stop was Vernon, Texas, for gas and something to eat. It had been a long drive from Amarillo. As I walked around the car, I noticed more blackness on the trunk, I checked the oil again, down at least a quart. Better go purchase a couple more quarts to carry in the trunk. The next stop was Wichita Falls, I didn't need any gas, some of the other guys did though, and I wanted to check the oil- again. Yep, another quart low. Now I'm really getting worried as to why the engine is burning so much oil and we're not even to our destination. I pulled the No.8 plug and it's fouled worse than before. I checked a couple plugs on that side, they didn't look all that clean. "Dave, can I have a couple of plugs?" I asked. "I'll replace 'em for you when we get to Denison.

When we got to Denison, I had gone through four quarts of oil and the engine needed another two quarts...and it's only 750 miles from Denver to Denison. Big problem now...will we be able to get back home with the engine using that much oil?

It took some work to get the blackness off the trunk but we had a great time at the kustom event, quite a few of us took home some of their awards. We left Sunday afternoon after the awards and headed back home on the same highway we took down - didn't want to take any county roads in case the engine in the '57 decided to go away at 70 mph. We stopped in Wichita Falls to check the oil and found no oil on the dipstick-it was all over the trunk of the car-so black the Mint Green color of the car didn't even show through. None of the guys we were running with wanted to follow us - they wanted to be in front - who could blame them? We had to wipe off the taillights a couple of times so drivers behind us could see our brake lights.

While some of our pals were eating at Long John Silver's, Dan and I went next door to Wal-Mart and bought two cases of their cheapest oil - no sense paying gasoline station quart prices when the engine was going through that much.

To make this whole story a bit shorter, we used 16 more quarts of oil and five new spark plugs between Wichita Falls and home. By the time we got home, the entire trunk and taillights were covered in black burnt oil so we knew the engine was toast. As we got closer to home we were surprised we were able to make it. FWIW, that car has never left us stranded on the side of the road.

Since the rod running season was over around ColoRODo, we garaged the car. About March we pulled the engine, made a trip to the Chevy dealer, purchased a new 350" crate motor and installed it. We gave the oil burner to a friend, he rebuilt it and put it in his '55-says it's a good engine now!

THE UFO INCIDENT

You've read about the Very Large Array in New Mexico and the supposed alien abductions around there in the White Mountains of Arizona in a previous story, but this incident occurred in eastern Arizona and shocked a couple of Arizona's finest.

November, 2000. Holbrook, New Mexico. That warm Sunday afternoon, after the awards, we cruised out of the Scottsdale , Arizona, Good-guys event and headed north, for home, close to 1000 miles away. East of Scottsdale, we grabbed Highway 87, a nice four lane up to Payson (about 50 miles). It's a great drive from the hot desert floor covered with giant cactus to the cool pine-covered mountains, but there's one really strange thing about that highway. Somewhere close to Payson, the road switches over the top of one another...meaning as you're going down toward Scottsdale, you're on the east side of the mountain looking to the right, across a valley, to see people going up. I think it's very unusual and I've never found another highway like it.

After a quick lunch/dinner in Payson, we took Highway 260, a two lane in most places, and aimed for Heber (60 miles distance) after that we'd take a narrow two-lane (Highway 377, about 40 miles), that'd hook us up to the Interstate at Holbrook. I say narrow cuz it's no more than a county road – curvy, ruff, up and down hills and across what was once a lake, now dry. We'd planned on spending the night in Gallup, depending on how long it took us to get there. After Payson, I turned off the A/C...it was beginning to get cool running through the pines. Anyway, I'm running the front door in the Mint Green radical '57, our pal, Dave Pareso is running second in his orange and flamed, chopped '51 Merc and Dan is last in line driving the gray '57. By the time we hit Highway 377, it's past sunset, and remember, this was mid-November...short days. The speed limit, if I remember correctly, was 55 through there...I'm running over 70, got the stereo going full blast - just cruising, enjoying the way the lowered '57 handles. As it got darker, I flipped on the park lights in the rad '57 – the '54 Chevy park lights are green cuz the whole car is Mint Green…then I think why not turn on the neon, too…in the open-mouthed grille…behind the '54 Chevy teeth. Get the picture? Two green "eyes" and a mouthful of green teeth…coming atcha fast and flying low to the ground.

Dan asked over the CB, "Park lights on?" seeing the bright red of the full width U-shaped taillights in the radical '57.

I acknowledge.

"And the neon?" he asked. I know he's grinning cuz he likes the look of it, too. "I'll turn on my park lights too." Now I'm grinning because the park lights in the gray '57 are behind the aluminum flat bar grille I'd built and nearly light up the whole grille.

"Of course," I answer. Dave says he'll turn on his park lights and under-car neon, a purple glow under the bright orange of the Merc.

We're headed up a small hill - I remembered that at the top of the hill, it levels and runs straight for a mile or two…I hit the top of the rise going a bit more than 75, the rock n' roll tuneage loud and I'm enjoying the ride. There, to my shock, to the right of the highway, there sits two Arizona Highway Patrolmen…one facing me, the other car's tail to me so he could talk to the other officer.

"Oh crap," I said out loud. Too late now, I've been had. No sense lifting.

As I scream by, my exhausts wailing, I see the patrolman facing me, his mouth agape…chin on the floor, eyes wide in shock… my low-flying, loud, green UFO surprised him, and is followed closely by another purple/orange low-flying UFO…and then followed by the Gray scout ship behind both…!!!

I look in the mirror -- the brake lights on the patrol car come on for just an instant and then blink out. I watch the rear view mirror as I scream north. The patrol car doesn't move…neither does the other one. I think that maybe they were too shocked to react.

The CB crackles – Dan is laughing. "Did you see the look on that officer's face?"

"I think he thought we were UFO's skimming the ground," Dave chuckled.

"They're not coming after us," Dan said. "...neither one has moved."

By that time, I'm half a mile past them and my speed is off a bit – scared me...and I thank my lucky stars they didn't pursue. I really think both of them couldn't believe what they just saw. I'd bet they're still telling the story about those 3 UFO's following a lonely highway and flying low around in the Arizona mountains these days.

About halfway to Holbrook, I turned on the heat...the darkness was dropping the outside temperatures-November, remember? Half hour later, the lights of Holbrook showed up from atop the hill as the highway led us down and I could see headlights on the Interstate. The park lights/neon grille were turned off and the headlights pulled on. We cruised slowly through town to the Interstate. No more than five, six miles past Holbrook, I've got the speed up to 75 again and some kind of screeching is coming from the '57's engine compartment. You know it had to be loud cuz I was rocking out, tuneage was really blasting...!!! I turned the stereo down, the noise got louder... I clutched it thinking the throw-out bearing was going away...nope, flip the ignition off...yep, alternator bearing, water pump bearing...some bearing is near gone out of something. I radioed Dan and Dave I'm pulling over.

Grab the flashlight, unlock the hood – hmmmm, shiny wet fluid covers everything...what is that? Not anti-freeze, car's not running hot. Nothing dripping under the radiator. Not oil either. Dave and Dan are beside me, we're all under the hood shinning the light around and wiping up the mess with paper towels trying to find out where it came from when this booming voice breaks the silence.

"Got a problem?"

Bonk! I hit my head on the hood straightening up.

An Arizona Highway Patrolman shines his flashlight over our faces.

"Ulp. Uhm. Yeah," I said, surprised we didn't see the headlights of his car pull up behind us. "But we don't know what it is. Loud screeching, can't figure it out. Uhm, I'll start it so we can hear it."

It started...turns out the screeching was the belt around the A/C compressor...seems the compressor bearing seized, froze up the pulley and blew fluid all over everything. The patrolman pulled out a 6 inch folding knife and handed it to me. "Cut the belt," he ordered, "you can replace it later. We need to get you guys moving."

"Uhm, yeah, sure!" I do as ordered, hand the belt to Dan and he wraps the soaked belt in paper towels...so far the patrolman hasn't said anything about us flying low outside of Heber...sure hope it isn't the same officer.

I closed the hood halfway, locked the padlock and shut it. "OK, good to go," I said as we all head for our cars. I was about to climb into the '57 when the patrolman stops by Dave's Merc, turns to me and points, "Oh, by the way, try to keep it under 90."

THE WYOMING INCIDENT

Short "weekend" trips we like. Not all of our rod running is long distance. This rod running trip took us north to Casper, Wyoming, about a four hour drive from our home.

May, 2001. Casper, Wyoming/Ft. Collins, ColoRODo. My bro, Dan, and I made a trip to Casper, Wyoming, 280 miles north of Denver, for the Oil Capital Auto Club's Memorial Day rod run/event. It was their first event and the first time we'd been to Casper as well. Dan took his '64 Super Sport we'd built for him a few years earlier and I drove the radical, chopped '57 Chevy. We left Friday morning, 110 miles later, we stopped for lunch in Cheyenne…130 miles north of Cheyenne, I started to hear grinding…sounded like a rear wheel bearing. Bad news: I've seen axles shear off at speed…wheel and tire exiting the wheel well, causing a severe accident and no telling how long this one would last. I radioed Dan, via the CB's we use and told him one of the rear wheel bearings was going and I'd slow down to prevent an accident but didn't know if I could make it to Casper. At 45 mph in the right lane, I wasn't much hindrance to traffic – besides, there wasn't much traffic going north anyway. The remaining 40 or so miles went by slowly. Over an hour later, we pulled into the outskirts of Casper and called our friend, Rick Thurston of Rick's Rod Shop, told him of our problem. He asked if I wanted to replace both rear wheel bearings, I acknowledged and he had the parts deliver them to his shop and we were on his hoist Saturday morn.

That close call wasn't bad…at least I had some warning…and the ruined bearing held up until we got on Rick's hoist on Saturday. We pulled the axles and installed both bearings while Rick and crew were doing safety NSRA inspections for the event.

The rest of the weekend, and the event itself, was great. We stayed over Sunday night, the 4-hour road trip back home would be Monday…Memorial Day.

My brother is never without a map..."There's a two-lane west of Casper, let's take a scenic route home." OK...I'm always up for a scenic tour since I hate driving Interstates! Over Rattlesnake Hills, through the Shirley Mountains and into the town of Medicine Bow. Then east to Laramie, grab a two-lane "shortcut" south- stay off the Interstate. Highway 287 is 60 miles of scenic mountain road, curves, cliffs, red rocks and evergreens. The plan was to catch Interstate 25 at Ft. Collins, ColoRODo, and run the remaining 75 miles home on four-lane. The drive from Laramie was uneventful until I motored down the I-25 on-ramp. Memorial Day, remember? I-25's loaded, it's the first holiday weekend of the year and it's Monday...and everyone's in a hurry to get home! Dan led, I followed.

OK, one hour to home...I'm tired...worst time in an automobile...attention span's short, getting home is high on the list. Dan punched his '64 up to 85 mph...merged with traffic. I clutched the 4-speed into third, nailed the accelerator and eased behind a pickup pulling a boat, running- according to my speedometer - 90 mph.

When I go through a town, I turn off the stereo...don't know why, I just do. Here I am, hurrying down the highway, keeping up with traffic and not even thinking of turning the stereo back on...in retrospect, I'm glad it was off. I'm in the inside lane –the 'fast' lane and I hear noise again...don't recognize it. Growling, then louder - rumbling. I lift my foot from the accelerator. First thing I think is that new rear wheel bearing is defective. I grabbed the CB mic, radio Dan, "Got a problem, gonna slow." Just as I said that, the '57 starts vibrating, but don't know where or what it's coming from. I don't panic or hit the brakes but visualized wheel/tire leaving the car, launching it, and I, into the center lane of traffic, causing a multi-car pile-up of great proportions and possibly killing someone...me, included! The back end of the car starts bouncing wildly, shaking almost uncontrollably, it was harder than hell to hold onto the steering wheel. I aimed for the shoulder. Aiming, at 60 mph, is the best I can do. The gyrations worsen...road's shoulder coming fast. I shifted down to third, try to keep the rear of the car from coming around. Forty mph, skid onto the shoulder, try to avoid roadway markers.

Naw, flatten them if necessary. Tap the brakes, the '57's rear continues to bounce. Horrendous bouncing. Good thing my seat belt is on. Pull into second gear, deduce now it's not wheel bearings – gotta be a tire coming off the rim! Car slows, bouncing slows. My heart doesn't. Ease the car to a halt, shut it off, unbuckle the seat belt, open the door and fall out, shaking. That was close. Too damned close in that kind of traffic.

By then, Dan had stopped and backed up on the shoulder- not exactly legal and dangerous in itself. He and I check the rear of the car to see…nothing! Tires and wheels are where they're supposed to be and both hold air. What the hell? Look under the car…nothing. Grab a screwdriver, remove passenger's side rear hubcap…two lug nuts fall out, then four. How'd they loosen? Hmmmmmmmmmm, the lug nuts haven't worked loose, it's the studs -- sheared off at the axle. Broken…lug nuts still attached. Four of 'em…busted…one lug nut/stud held the wheel/tire on, wouldn't have lasted much longer either, it showed signs of serious wear-metal on metal. Check the other side, it's OK, pull the 'caps from the fronts, they're OK too. I'd just escaped a major holiday accident. Why?

I didn't care at that point. I thanked my God just the same…and my guardian angel.

I got out the small hydraulic jack we always carry and instructed Dan to go find the nearest exit, turn around or take the next two-lane going west he comes across and drive back into Ft. Collins, find the only auto parts store open and buy studs/lug nuts. I pulled the drum, punched out what was left of the studs out of the axle with a hammer and screwdriver while he's gone. By the time I'm done, he's back, I slip new studs into place, pull them into the axle with washers, lug nuts and lug wrench, put the wheel back on, tighten the nuts and let the car down. The first few blocks I drove on the shoulder, not exactly certain that solved the problem…it did, so we eased back onto the highway and drove for home, at 50 mph, in rain. Best part-we'd avoided a major hail-storm just north of Denver that we would have driven right into if we had not broken down.

Would you call it dumb luck? I don't, anymore!

Over the years I've become convinced it's more than that...I believe someone unseen rides with me...a guardian angel...and believe me when I tell you I didn't believe in such things way back when I first started driving. Perhaps you don't believe in such things, maybe you do...either way, it's OK. I do, now, and I'm certain it's my guardian angel simply because he, or she has saved us more than once! Yet, I don't know who it is or why they keep me safe...how else can I explain the fact that both Dan and I have gotten out of nearly every close encounter we've ever had over 40-some years of driving the nation's highways and we are still here, to tell these stories?

I cannot, at least, I believe in it and that's what is important to me!

THE DILLON INCIDENT

Kustom guru Bo Huff had personally invited Dan and I to attend his car show in Sunnyside, Utah so we drove both our kustoms. Sunnyside is about an eight hour drive from our home. This incident happened on the way back home.

July, 2001. Wolcott, Colorado. There we were, cruising down the highway. I had the tunes turned up high just enjoying the music, when the CB crackled to life. "Hey Dan, I got a problem," Roger called over the airwaves. "Try and find someplace to pull over, will you?"

Whoa. Let's stop here and back up to the beginning of this trip.

Dan and I had driven over to Sunnyside, Utah, to attend the Community Daze Car Show on Friday. We were invited to attend this show by Bo Huff, who lived in nearby Dragerton. Roger drove the radical Mint Green '57 Chevy Hardtop and Dan cruised his '90's custom '64 Chevy Impala SS. Then on Saturday we spent most of the day at Bo's general store/museum hanging out looking at all his cool stuff and listening to the bands play.

Sunday was the show. We had a great time in the Sunnyside Park, checking out the other participant's (mostly kustom) cars and listening to more bands play. That afternoon the awards were held (we each won one) and we headed for home after the show ended. We had a six hour drive ahead of us, and knew that we would arrive home late evening, in the dark.

We caught I-70 at Green River and headed East towards Grand Junction. We got gas just outside of Grand Junction and got back on the Interstate to Glenwood Springs and the canyon. Driving out of the big cut in the mountain, past Gypsum and Eagle, near Wolcott is where I called Dan on the CB. Since Dan usually leads on our trips, "Pull-out coming right up," he said. We stopped at a scenic spot right along the Interstate and I got out to check the right front tire. He got the jack out of the trunk, jacked it up to check the wheel bearing. Yep, it wobbled. Bearing is going or nearly gone.

"Take the next exit and find a parts store, if possible and if one is still open," he said as we got back on the highway. Well, there happened to be a NAPA store not far from where we stopped so we whipped into their parking lot. When we got out of our cars, I told Dan the right front wheel bearing was bad and this was a good place to stop! Went inside to the parts guy behind the counter, told him our problem and could we fix the situation in his lot?

"Do you need a bearing?" he asked.

"Don't know yet until we get the drum off the spindle," Dan said. So we jacked up the front and pulled the wheel and drum off, but the bearing was stuck on good. Out came the tool box with the pliers and big hammer. "Might have to chisel the bearing off to fit a new one," I said so Dan went inside to buy a package of five flat bladed chisels and brought them out. I started beating on the bearing with the chisel trying to cut a groove in the bearing race to try and spin the bearing around to get it off. The first chisel tip started to break away in small pieces, not affecting the race at all. Another chisel and a few more blows to the race and that chisel end disintegrated, too. We went through that whole package and each chisel wasn't worth a crap. Dan took them back in the store and got his money back. Cheap Chinese junk!

After beating on the bearing for over an hour, I decided to put the drum and wheel back on and head down the road towards home, not too certain how far we'd get. So, back on the highway and we drove to Frisco, another 36 miles. We'd made it over Vail Pass (elevation 10,666 ft.) and Copper Mountain but we stopped at the Dillon Lake Overlook just past the Frisco exit to let the front bearing cool down before trying to get up to Eisenhower Tunnel. By now the sun was starting to set and it was going to get dark soon. We again got back on the highway and got a little closer to home, but then I called Dan via the CB and told him we weren't going to make it to the tunnel. "The bearing is really screeching and I don't want to be stuck on the side of the road up there when the bearing gets completely disintegrated, so, let's get off at Silverthorne and find a motel for the night. We'll figure out how to fix it in the morning."

We exited and found a Days Inn and pulled into the lot. After considerable conversation about what to do and how to fix the situation we got a room. Man, we were only two hours from home and we really didn't want to spend the night here. But what choice do we have?

"Wonder what Ron Brown is doing?" I asked. We called our friend Ron to see if he could come and get us with his trailer. By that time it's 9 PM. Sure enough he wasn't doing anything that Sunday evening. He said stay there (like we weren't going anywhere anyway!) and he'd come and rescue us. So we went to the motel desk clerk and told her our sad story. She cancelled our room for us and gave us our money back.

At eleven-thirty we were waiting outside and Ron rolled into the lot with his Ford F-350 diesel pickup and enclosed twenty- foot trailer. Our good friend to the rescue! We got the '57 loaded, tied down and headed for home. On the climb up long hill to the tunnel, Dan's in the lead in his '64, holding the pedal to the metal trying to gain speed when Ron flew by Dan like he was standing still. That Ford diesel wasted no time climbing that mountain. Dan followed him all the way home and was impressed how that truck performed loaded with a car in the trailer. Nothing slowed him down, not even coming down out of the foothills, which can be tricky at times.

By the time we got home and unloaded the car it was one-thirty AM. The wheel bearing had to be cut off with a plasma cutter later in the week but it got healed up and to this day, that bearing is still on the car!

THE GALLUP INCIDENT

Dan and I like to go to Scottsdale in November. It's a lot warmer down there than it is in Denver, however, getting there sometimes is tuff and it's usually cold on the way until we get past Prescott, Arizona. We'd asked one of our car pals to go with us this time and this story is more about his car than one of ours.

November, 2001. Western, New Mexico. Heading for Good-guys Scottsdale event from Denver, we planned to over-night in Gallup, NM. We'd been driving all day and it got dark, cold, too...especially in the mile high desert. I'm in the rad '57 Chevy hardtop, my bro is in the Gray '57 Chevy - and our pal, Dave Pareso (and GF, Chris), in his chopped '51 Merc. My heater is on full blast, I'm warm, the stereo is cranking and the CB is turned up so I can hear it over the tuneage. We're running I-40 about 75 per, not a care in the world, other than getting hungry.

We usually don't have highway troubles...Dan and I keep our cars in good shape for that reason, but this trip it caught up with Dave.

He's running last in our 3-some...Dan is at the front cuz I like to follow and check out scenery...I glanced in the mirror and noticed Dave is gone. Just then I hear "Just lost fire, engine is dead."

I yelled at Dan...he'd heard and headed for the shoulder. Dave is back about a quarter mile, out of the Merc, hood up.

After pulling a plug wire off the hot engine, he said, "Chris, try to start it."

Nothing...the engine doesn't wing over, no spark coming out of the plug.

"Coil die?" I asked, after backing up.

"Amp meter take a crap?" Dan asked next

"Internal coil-HEI, more than likely," Dave said. "Happened before. I've got a spare."

Good thing too, the sooner we get off the Interstate, the better. Dave popped the trunk, piled traveling stuff on the roadway...finally found where it's stashed. "Uhm, not there. Guess I left the spare back home."

"We've got a tow strap," Dan said. "Tow you into Gallup or Rog or I can go back to Grants for parts…we're about halfway between."

"Let's tow, no sense going back," Dave said. "How far?"

"Twenty miles. You can handle that on the end of a tow strap?"

"Yeah," Dave said. "But Chris can't. Without heat in the Merc, she'll freeze."

"She can ride with me," I said. Dan opened his trunk and fished out the 10 foot tow strap. He hooked it to the frame of the Gray '57 and strung it back to the Merc, attached it to the frame under Dave's '55 Pontiac split bumper. The ten foot tow strap allowed seven, eight feet between …not much, but enough - "if we don't run 75." Dave cautioned.

Starting slowly at first until both are comfortable with the short tow strap, I take the front in case we come upon something in the road. Besides, Dave's Merc has power brakes and they don't work well without power. At about 55, vehicles are whizzing by like we're standing still. No matter, in the high desert there ain't much to see, and when dark - nothing! No city lights, no moonshine, no distant mountains to break the horizon, nothing but headlights coming at us, taillights passing.

I kept an eye on the mirror, watched in case Dan flashes his lights if he has a problem, I can't get too far ahead. Once I thought I saw a flash of light, like lightning. Wasn't headlights, though. Starry out, must be seeing things. I called on the CB, "You just see a flash of light?"

"Yeah, I did, thought I was seeing things, but not if you saw it too."

"Eighteen wheeler, shooting pictures of us," Dave said.

About that time the tractor pulled even with Dan, he turned to look and got flashed, right in his eyes, "Damn, that's bright."

"You OK to keep going?"

"Yeah, but don't look out your window when he gets alongside."

Seconds later the huge truck pulls even. After several flashes he goes past and I see his passenger's side window is up. "Get this," I said, "he's shooting pics through his side window...surely the flash bounced back?" We all got a good chuckle...I could just hear him when he's going through his pictures later, "What the hell are these and where was this...???" Surely he got pictures of himself reflected in the window!

We pulled into a gas station in Gallup about 8:30 PM ...found out that the auto parts stores are next exit, a couple miles...and they close at 9.

Chris and I park next to the Merc, the '57's heater running full blast cuz it's cold ...both cars gather lots of lookie-lou's...'course, what chopped, orange, multi-color flamed Merc wouldn't, especially with a radical, chopped Mint Green'57 Bel Air sitting alongside? We keep rolling windows up and down to answer questions.

Forty-five minutes later the gray '57 rolls in...hopefully they've got the parts needed...if not, we'll figure something out.

Half hour later the Merc fires, idles on its own...we're all starving and time to find a motel...oh sure, next exit, figures! We check in, however, there's no restaurants close, have to go back an exit...forget it...order pizza. Dave tells us he never wants to be on the end of a 6 foot tow strap again because all he can see through his chopped windshield is gray '57 Chevy fins...!!! We hit the sack, look forward to warm Scottsdale tomorrow afternoon.

End of story, right...??? Not quite...

Figure we'd leave at 7, grab something to eat on the way and get into sunny warm Scottsdale about 2. The ol' Merc has other ideas...Dave left his park lights on last night while unloading the trunk...battery is dead...electric doors won't pop... electric trunk won't open. I finished scraping the frost off the windows with a credit card. "Jump it?" I asked.

"Maybe," Dave said...so, gray '57 to the rescue...again...jumper cables out, Dave hooked 'er up. The engine groaned and finally fired...he popped the door and then the trunk...the car idled while they load. We hit the highway about 8:30, the temp was 20 degrees. Dan is running the front door, Dave is second and I'm last in line this time. Seems no more than 10 minutes at highway speed when Dave yells over the CB.

"Got a problem, pulling over."

He coasted to the side of the road and I see a long trail of liquid under the Merc...smoking too...uh-oh, could be a major problem...by the time I'm stopped, Dave is under the front of his car.

"Major problem?" I asked.

"Tranny line popped off the cooler." Dave said. "But I don't have any fluid, I looked last night...I forgot everything this trip."

None of us had tranny fluid. Dan drove several miles back into town to get some. Meantime, Dave put the line on and tightened both clamps. By the time Dan returned, we were cold, again. Dave filled the tranny and we started...the heaters going full blast, even though the sun is bright.

We rolled into Scottsdale about 3 and everything seemed to be OK...Friday, the gray car started acting up...we replaced points and condenser toward the cooler part of the evening and it ran fine. So far, two cars have acted up...hope the rad '57 doesn't...it usually doesn't, it's a good car.

We had a great time that weekend, got to see lots of cars we don't normally see and enjoyed summer-like weather. We headed for home Sunday after checking out the award winners.

End of this story, right? Well, no, not exactly...

THE LONLIEST HIGHWAY IN THE WORLD INCIDENT

This one was one of the few long distance trips we'd taken in a while. Dan and I like to stay off the Interstates as much as possible and like to find two-lane highways. Highway 50 across Nevada is a two-lane.

May, 2002. Carson City, Nevada. We'd been to Paso Robles weekend kustom car event and spent some time driving around Morro Bay and along the coast. I was driving the radical Mint Green '57 Chevy and Dan was driving the Gray '57 two door. After Morrow Bay, we went back up through Paso and up over the hill, headed for home. We took a lonely two lane that we thought was a state highway toward Creston. It wasn't, but that was OK, because we like "lonely highways." Someone, somewhere, sometime ago had told us Highway 50 across Nevada was the "Loneliest Highway in the World" and that it's known for its remoteness. It looked like our kinda highway on the map - stretching straight across the Nevada desert from Carson City. Driving desert never bothered us either...so we pointed our kustoms for Tahoe.

It took us a couple of days to get across Cali and north to Sacramento. We took Highway 50 up to Tahoe and stayed over-night in Tahoe. In the morning, we wound down the mountain to Carson City and found Highway 50...we passed Fallon Naval Air Station, never have figured out why there is a Naval Air Station in a desert, but I assume the government, in its infinite wisdom knows much more about that than I do (come to find out it's a training airfield that has been the home of the U.S. Navy's Naval Strike and Air Warfare Center including the TOP GUN training program since 1996. It was moved from Naval Air Station Miramar after that air station transferred to the U.S. Marine Corp - Google is your friend). We also drove by (I think) the Mustang Ranch and questioned why anyone would raise horses in the desert? I've since found out it wasn't horses, but much more like "horsing around" there. So much so that I'm not so sure that part of Highway 50 is, in fact, "the loneliest highway in the world," let alone that part of Nevada as there was lots of traffic around that ranch...(Who's your friend? Google told me the Mustang Ranch is closer to Reno so I don't know the name of the "Ranch" we passed).

Anyway, Highway 50 runs 305 miles across Nevada, about a six hour trip for us before we hit the Utah border. The highway isn't really straight, nor is it flat...Highway 50 crosses nine mountain ranges that run north and south and they aren't simply up and down - the roadway is typical of any mountain road, curvy with switchbacks as the road climbs to the summit. The mountain ranges aren't high mind you, nothing like the 10,000 or 11,000 foot passes in ColoRODo. The highest pass on Highway 50 is 7722 feet- 'Conner's Pass,' on the eastern edge of the state...the lowest is 6340 feet- 'New Pass Summit' on the western side of Nevada, just east of Fallon Naval Air Station.

South of there, down toward Las Vegas, Nellis Air Force base has a "range" (great open area-not mountain range!) that appears to be about 5000 square miles of 'restricted airspace.' An additional 7,700 miles of airspace north and east of that restricted range is also available for military flight operations over some 3 million acres. We assumed that's where the fighters came from. WHAT fighters, you ask? Well, read on...

We were minding our own business, driving along, enjoying the sights and smells since we had all the windows down climbing the ranges when, somewhere east of Fallon, we passed a sign close to the top of the summit that stated "Beware low flying aircraft."

"Hmmmmm, okay," I said to Dan over the CB, "how low can they get?" We bantered back and forth about what type of airplane would be flying low over these ranges when we decided it had to be F-14's, maybe F-15's since the Navy and Air Force flew both. The conversation drifted around to how many more mountain ranges we had to cross before we got to Utah and we'd forgotten about the 'low flying aircraft' sign.

The roar of jet engines woke us right up…two fighters screamed directly over the top of us, I swear no more than three feet above. The canopies glistening in the sunlight as the nimble gray jets screeched over the top of us and the pass and dived directly for the desert floor. So close I could count the number of rivets on the underside of the wings and saw exactly what kind of ordnance they carried on their way to the Bravo 20 bombing range, which is equipped with dummy power plants , refineries, bridges and highways used for practice bomb runs (Googled it!). I really don't know if that's where they were headed and they really weren't just three feet above us, it just felt that way – the '57 Chevy actually vibrated from the engine noise. Scared me! I didn't have to tell Dan, via the CB to pull over, he was already stopped and out of the car. By the time I got pulled over and grabbed the camera, they were already a good distance from us so I couldn't see any markings on them to tell if they were Air Force or Navy fighters.

Back in the car and headed for the next mountain range across the valley floor, I speculated that those pilots simply wanted to get a closer look at those 'two cool old cars down there on the highway climbing the ranges.' We crossed the next mountain range, drove across the valley and were chatting on the CB about the 'close call' we'd had and how unusual that was when we started up the next mountain range. I commented to Dan that I thought we were now far enough from Fallon that we probably wouldn't see any more of those fighter jets. Just as I finished that statement and clicked off the CB, the same scream of low flying jet aircraft engines shook the '57. Scared me…again! Buzzing me once I could see, and understand – I mean I was crossing a military training area…but to do it to me twice was just a bit much…I'm a taxpayer…and IF I can't get a ride in one of those things, WHY did they have to entice me by buzzing me…twice, at over 190,000 miles an hour? Not nice! Dan and I pulled off the road near the top of the summit and waited. Waited and watched, craning our necks around like our heads were on furniture swivels, absolutely daring any of those pilots to come screaming around again so we could get some swell close-up photos.

123

Dan finally turned the camera off and tossed it on the seat of his '57. "Maybe they're done with their bombing runs for the day?"

"Guess so," I said, "and we still have a couple hundred miles to cover yet...wouldn't mind getting to Delta, Utah, yet today, and that's 90 miles past the state line."

On the west side of Ely, Nevada, we about plowed into a herd of black cattle browsing alongside and on the highway. At that time it was past dusk and getting darker. How those cows got outside the fenced area I don't know but when the sunlight goes away behind the mountain ranges and all the cattle are black, it's hard to see them. After that little scare, we cruised just a bit slower and pulled into Delta, Utah past dark-thirty looking for a motel.

While this isn't exactly a break-down story, we thought a road trip kinda experience would be interesting. Hope you enjoyed it.

THE HEARTLAND INCIDENT

Another one of our long weekend trips. This one had been planned since January and that's when we initially plan our trips. That's the best time to plan as motel reservations can be made at any motel in January for the rest of the year.

July, 2002. Des Moines, Iowa. It was nearing the Fourth of July and Dan and I decided to head east for Des Moines and the Good-guys Heartland Nats. We hadn't been to that event in several years and there were no other shows around the Denver area July 4th weekend, so we decided to load up the radical '57 Chevy that I'd drive and Dan would drive his custom '64 Impala SS. (Yes, Dan has had that '64 a long time...matter of fact, he and I just finished a two week trip to Seattle, Washington, in the summer of 2017 and you can read about that story as the last of the 'incident' stories herein).

We planned to overnight in the Omaha area and then to Des Moines the next day, Thursday, catch the kick-off party at the host hotel that evening. Well, not being confined to any type of schedule, we took the Interstate about 30 miles east of Denver and grabbed Highway 36, a two-lane. We crossed into Kansas, drove to Oberlin and went north. We found some little traveled two-lanes across southern Nebraska ending up in Beatrice. We didn't make Omaha but found a motel there and stayed over-night. Both of us like to travel different roads and some of these highways we'd never been on.

After breakfast, we continued east and crossed the Missouri River into Iowa and started stepping our way up to Des Moines from southeast Iowa. Just after crossing the river, Roger radioed that the '57 was jerking like it had an electrical issue. We pulled over and opened the hood to check things out. Seeing nothing really wrong, I checked the coil...it was quite hot for some reason —could be the cause of the problem. Dan said he had another coil in the trunk of the '64 and went to get it. We swapped the coils and started the car.

125

Seemed fine so we set out again. The new coil made the difference and the car didn't jerk anymore.

We made it to the kick-off party Thursday night and the show on Friday was full of lots of nice cars. The De Moines fairground is huge if you've never been there and the grounds has city streets running through it...it's almost like regular city blocks but there are plenty of open buildings for cows, pigs, chickens and the like to be displayed. Iowa is, after all, a farming state and farmer's like to show off their pride. It was actually crowded and both Dan and I were wondering where the cars that come in on Saturday were going to park.

We found out as we cruised in on Saturday morn. It took us about half an hour to get into the ground as we were required to get off the street and cruise back and forth on an empty grass lot until such time as we made it to the front of the line and onto the main street of the grounds. Needless to say, by the time we got onto the asphalt, the car was dusty! There were absolutely no parking spots available on the main street and people were parking their cars in the empty sheep barns, pig sheds and horse corrals. Needless to say, I think every rod and kustom from the Mid-West had shown up.

As we were cruising around looking for a good parking spot, the '57 started acting up again. We eventually found a place to park both our cars on one of the side streets (no pig sheds for us!). We checked the coil again and it was very hot...this time we'd only driven from the hotel to the grounds, only a few miles. We swapped out the coils but it didn't make any difference this time. It seemed the timing was off causing the car to start but die right away. Could the timing chain have slipped? A few guys wandered by and after seeing the hood up on the '57 asked what the problem was and of course, each guy offered a different solution to the problem. Finally an old acquaintance, Ron Offerson from Denver came by and asked what the problem was. We explained and he offered to take a look at it, suggesting that maybe the problem was the Pertronix unit in the distributor. Roger had never heard of Pertronix having problems like that but he and Roger pulled the distributor. The electronics were burnt. Now what? Dan remembered that we'd kept all the original parts in the trunk so Ron and Roger set on a park bench and rebuilt the distributor with the old points and condenser. Ron slipped the distributor back in, found top dead center and had Roger fire it up. The engine sounded a lot better, no miss and it stayed running. Ron set the timing by ear and that was it. We thanked him and he went back to his car.

We enjoyed the rest of the day now that the car was fixed and we could get back home! Dan and I very seldom sit behind our cars at a show because we like walking around looking at all the variety of rods and kustoms at a large event like this one.

As the day wound down, we wanted to make a pass around the grounds to show off our cars. We picked up our chairs to put them in the trunk ...but...the trunk of the '57 wouldn't open. What the hell-did the '57 decide it didn't want to be here and is giving us fits? The switch didn't seem to work, wouldn't release the trunk. We checked the wires going into the switch and they seemed fine. We even tried using direct current from the battery to the switch to open it but even that didn't work. Dan suggested using the battery from his '64 to power the trunk solenoid, took the battery out of his '64 and set it on the floor of the '57 and ran some wire but even that didn't work.

OK, how can we get in the trunk-can't remove the rear bucket seats cuz they are bolted in. Frustrated with the '57 we were about to forget putting the chairs in the trunk of the '57 and put them in the trunk of the '64 and head back to the motel when Dan remembered we'd added an emergency "trap door" to the trunk floor of the '57. Roger crawled under the car, opened the hatch and had to move some stuff out of the way so he could get his arm inside. A couple of minutes of wiggling the trunk release and the trunk opened. While we had it open we played with the switch figuring the switch had gone bad but that wasn't the case at all. It worked fine when the trunk was open. Roger got out his wrenches and proceeded to loosen the trunk latch. We took all of the stuff out of the trunk, he grabbed a flashlight and crawled in. "Dan, you close the trunk and then try the switch, I'll see what it's doing or not doing." Couple of times of adjusting the latch and opening and closing the trunk, the switch worked again. Apparently the bolts holding the solenoid on had slipped, kinda cocking the mechanism and not allowing it to be released. After that we've never had another problem with the trunk releasing. We got to cruise around the grounds and then went to find something to eat. Later that evening we came back to the grounds to watch the fireworks. Sunday morning we headed for home, a 10 hour drive. Unfortunately, we haven't been back to the GG's Des Moines event since!

THE MISSOURI INCIDENT

Let me preface this by saying I believe someone keeps my brother and I alive out on the highways and byways of this wonderful country - there are two possible 'guardians' watching over us: my Aunt Laura, who loved us two "boys" dearly. She passed away in 1996 at the age of 97 ... and the other guardian would be our Dad who passed away way too early at age 52.

August, 2005. Joplin, Missouri. Even though Dad and I didn't get along well after I got my driver's license, my younger brother, Dan was his favorite son. Dad passed away too early in 1966 at 52 years of age. Dad was a gear-head from the word 'go' and I learned a lot from him.

Anyway, the weekend of the third HAMB drags, for Dan and I, began at 6:30 AM Thursday as we headed out of Denver…fourteen uneventful hours later we pulled into Joplin, Missouri.

Our anticipation ran high for Friday and Saturday…and it would start Friday morning- an 8AM trip to the Springfield swap meet…so, we retired at 11:30 PM, it'd been a long day of riding in our hot rods.

Friday morn came way too fast…but we got in line for Springfield …Denise and Rudy led the procession to the swap meet, about an hour from Joplin.

It looked like rain all day, but held off…Dan and I headed back to Joplin about 5PM…and since I hate Interstates and its traffic, I asked my bro, who is never without a map, to find a different route…took old Highway 66 all the way to Carthage…saw several interesting sites along the way which provided great photo ops. Friday evening we hung out in the Ramada lot, watching more and more rods arrive for the Saturday drags.

Saturday morn was the Route 66 cruise…there was a line when we rolled into the lot…a very cool route had been laid out and we saw lots of interesting sites…about 50 cars participated in the cruise. We ended up in Red Oak II, the "community" artist Lowell Davis founded...full of metal sculpture, old buildings, houses and old cars.

Then it was back to the Ramada...about 3:30 that afternoon we headed out for the Mo-Kan track...by the time we arrived the place was already rocking! The pits were packed, had a hard time finding a spot...but soon took the Studey and my bro's '47 Chevy Aerosedan onto the track to see what they'd do.

The old Studey ran hard all night and could fry the whitewalls on that new concrete pad...turned in my best time at the next to the last run...and trying to haul down that car from 100 mph for the fast approaching return road and not go into the corn field required pulling it into second gear to slow and pump the brakes in order to make the turn. I don't know how those guys in the 413" Gilmore rail job slowed from the 130's...must have been a real handful!

The evening went by waaaaaaayyyy tooooooo fast and before we were ready, it was over...as the lights were turned out, we jumped into our rods and headed for the motel, a twenty mile ride...at the last traffic light just before turning into the motel lot I heard a 'snap' and felt the brake pedal give a little shudder...uh-oh, don't like the feel of that. I eased the Stude into the motel lot and decided it was too late to get a flashlight out to crawl under the car to check it. We hung around for a while, listened to stories of epic "old style" drag racing and retired just after midnight. We'd planned on leaving for home early morn.

In the morn I checked the Stude's brakes, found the brake pedal had broken its bolt and needed replacing...the original had been stripped out...can't go home without some way to apply the brakes...called up friend to see if he had parts. "Bring it over and we'll see what we can do." Jim C. lived in Webb City, about a twenty minute ride from the Ramada...jump in the Studey and head out...after going about ten blocks, a traffic light turns red...step on the brake to slow...uh-oh, ain't none! Got a real problem now! Pull emergency brake, flip a U-turn slowly and crawl back to the motel. After inspection I see driver's side rear wheel has fluid all over the tire - rear brake cylinder gone.

Have I ever mentioned that someone watches over me (and my bro) on these trips? I'd just spent Saturday on a 100 mile scenic cruise and Saturday night racing...flogging the old Stude through 8 low fifteen second quarters and trying to slow at the end of the strip from near 100 mph...and then I drove back to the motel from the strip, another twenty miles, half of it in Saturday night Joplin traffic...and the brake pedal gives up...to warn me of impending doom should I continue. It's really strange that happened in the last block...do I trust my unseen rider?

It took a few hours to find parts Sunday morn, put the car on a jackstand (yes, we always carry a hydraulic jack and a jackstand!) pull the drum then wheel cylinder off, put a new cylinder on, refill the master cylinder and bleed the brakes...Jim C. eventually drove up looking for us...unfortunately, we were so engrossed in getting the Studey fixed, we neglected to call him and tell him we were not getting to his place!

We replaced the brake pedal's broken bolt with a smaller bolt/nut (it'd hold until we got home) and tested the brakes in the lot - they work now! After a shower and lunch, we left Joplin at 2 PM - Salina, Kansas, would be as close to home as we could get before dark. It took a few miles before I was satisfied we weren't going to have more trouble with the brakes and took Highway 69 to Fort Scott. From Ft. Scott, we decided to take another route home so chose a couple of highways we hadn't been on...good thing we did...if we had taken Highway 400 as originally planned across Kansas we'd have gotten into the biggest rain & hail storm Wichita (and parts east of there) had had all year (according to the Wichita TV news we watched)...almost 3 inches in an hour. We would have driven right into the middle of it...don't think my Rain-X could have handled that...Wichita had a lot of flooding around the city cuz of all the rain. We watched Wichita's storm build from a distance of about 60 miles north of it and pulled into Salina at 8:30 PM and grabbed a motel.

It's usually an 8 hour run for us from Salina home, we hit the road at 8 AM Monday morn...I hate Interstates, remember? I prefer two-lanes - found one an hour south of Salina and pulled into Denver a little before 6... never ran in a bit of rain and it was hot all the way!

Plenty of "proof" in this story that someone watches over us…and regardless of who watches over us on our cross-country trips, I'm here to tell you that I am forever grateful!

THE PRAIRIE INCIDENT

This is a continuation of the previous story - yes, sometimes incidents happen more than once on a long distance trip!

August, 2005. LaCross, Kansas. It had been a long day's drive, actually over 13 hours of steady driving and we arrived in Joplin late afternoon Thursday. The HAMB drags was the reason we'd come and they'd start tomorrow-Friday. In the parking lot of the motel were lots of gassers, regular street driven coops and sedans of the 30s and 40's. Of course, 50's sedans were there too. The drags at the strip weren't going to happen until Saturday, but cars and people were showing up early.

In the morning, a scenic 'cruise' was scheduled and we didn't want to miss that. The only thing we needed to decide was which car we should drive-Roger's '40 Stude Coop or Dan's '47 Chevy Aerosedan. The cruise would follow Old Route 66 through Joplin and Carthage and into Springfield, approximately 70 miles from Joplin. Reason is there was a large swap meet there that day and we spent most of the day at the swap meet. After a full day of driving and walking the swap meet we headed back to Joplin.

By the time we got back to the motel Friday late, the lot was already full of more arrivals, eager for the drags the next morning. Anticipation was high so the parking lot party lasted well into the morning hours but not us, we hit the beds in our room about midnight.

The Mo-Kan Dragway was 20 miles from our motel, in the middle of a cornfield...which by this time of the year the corn was about 6 feet tall. It was hard to see the strip for the tall corn. By the time we got there around noon, there were already plenty of cars in the pit area. The first of the 'fun runs" was scheduled for around 3pm so we walked the pits and looked at cars. When the call came for staging, both Dan and I pulled our cars to the lanes and got ready to "race" each other. This was like regular drag racing with a full tree-stage light, 3 amber bulbs, a green and a red. Since Roger had a 400 ci small block in this Stude and me a lowly 350 ci , Roger smoked Dan right from the green light. Roger ran a 15.5 quarter and 98 mph...trying to stop from that speed to make the return road was a little tuff since the shut-off area was short. He had to drop the Studey into second and pump the brakes in order to slow enough to make the turn. Dan's sedan ran a17.50 quarter at about 80.

The races lasted until 10pm and by the time we'd gotten back to the motel, the parking lot was already full-lots of after-racing partying going on so it was hard to find a parking spot for the night. The day had been a complete blast. It's just too bad it was so far from Denver, otherwise we'd be doing it every year.

After fixing the brakes, we headed north on two-lanes for a while, then west, skirting around a massive late afternoon thunderstorm south in Wichita. We made it to Salina and decided to spend the night there.

Monday morning, we found a two-lane going west and took it. We both dislike driving Interstates so a two-lane is prime driving for us, we enjoy going through small towns on the way. About three hours out of Salina, Dan called on the CB, said he had a growling sound coming from the rear of the car and he didn't know what it was. We stopped and traded cars so I could try to figure out what it was. Deduced it was a rear wheel bearing going bad –won't make it the rest of the way home on that! We were just east of the small town of LaCross, Kansas, maybe we can find a parts store there that can press on a new bearing for us...and that's always a difficult find on the road-very few places have that capability, but it can be done. Sure enough, A NAPA store was in town-seems there's always a NAPA store in nearly every small town that farmer's depend on. We asked if they could do a rear wheel bearing for a '57 Chevy rear end and they said they couldn't get it in until tomorrow, but they'd have to order it. We thanked them for that and said we always carry a spare so don't need it, just need it removed and pressed on. They couldn't do it immediately but there was a farm equipment store east of town (we'd passed it) and the guy was a hot rodder - had a few nice cars. We pulled into the lot and found out the owner was at lunch. Not having a choice, we decided to go get lunch ourselves. When we got back he was there, we asked if he could press the bearing on, he said sure but we'd have to pull the axle ourselves. That's no problem for us. He volunteered his shop-had us move the car inside out of the heat and sun. He let us use the big shop jack and we pulled tire, drum and axle in a few minutes. The axle bearing was taken off and the new one pressed on. A half hour later the car was back together. As we thanked him we learned about his collection of Fords and looked at several pictures in his office – he owned several mid-60s hardtops with big engines. He also invited us to come down for their 'show' in mid-March and to this day we get flyers announcing their event. Unfortunately, we've never made it back there. By the time we left LaCross, it was late afternoon and it took us another 5 hours to get home, arriving just before it got dark.

THE HOOD INCIDENT, TWO

IF you've been keeping up on all these "Incidents," you'll remember reading about Dan, and his hood flying up on his '47 Chevy in Montana way back in May, 1986. Well, from that day on, we'd devised a way to keep the hoods closed on all our cars instead of relying on the secondary latch older cars used (and abused!). We use plastic covered cable, cable stops, two old Chevy U-joint bolts and a padlock. One end attached to the pan, the other attached and padlocked to the hood. Holds the hood shut and works every time. But on this trip, our good friend, Ron Brown, had just purchased his Cadillac and didn't know much about it. He's since fixed his hood like ours.

June, 2006. Idalia, ColoRODo. Our good friend, Ron Brown had just traded his '37 Chevy sedan for a- a '55 Ford F100 and a '56 Cadillac hardtop (with a Caddy 500" engine) and 'we' were in a "tour" heading to Oberlin, Kansas, some 240 miles from Denver for a car show.

Fourteen rods and customs were cruising Highway 36, a two-lane, running, as we usually do, just past the speed limit on the eastern plains of ColoRODo. We were approaching mile marker 221, 10 miles shy of the Kansas border.

Ron's Caddy was in the # 10 spot in our little caravan, towards the back...I'm one car behind him in the radical '57 and two other cars are behind me. My brother, Dan was leading the procession nine cars ahead of Ron.

As is typical for eastern ColoRODo in late May/early June, the wind was blowing quite hard- kinda hard on the gas mileage and the skies were cloudy, but we were only knocking down 240 miles, a little over one tank of gas.

Ron had been listening to the tunes in his '56 Cad and enjoying his A/C, not paying much attention to the big Caddy's hood bouncing since the car was new to him, he thought it was just normal for the big hood…a huge gust of wind moved the cars ahead of him to the edge of the road and Ron rolled into it. That huge gust of wind whipped under his hood, lifted it and wiggled the secondary catch off its latch…it flew open, wrapping itself across the windshield, smacking the roof and then stood straight up, making it impossible to see where he was going…and at 65 mph, that's not a good thing!

I was paying attention (my guardian angel…???) and saw the hood come up, brake lights illuminate…I slammed on mine to avoid the car in front of me who was braking hard…and then looked in my rear view mirror to see if the rest were paying attention…we all avoided a rear end collision …and each other. Ron had to stick his head out the side window to see where he was going, but safely came to a stop alongside the road. Several of the lead vehicles didn't see what happened and they motored on. I called Dan on the CB we always have in our cars to let him know what happened and Dan got everyone stopped and waited for us. Several cars came back to find us and see what happened.

By the time they got there, three of us had already gotten tools out and began to remove the damaged hood…no other damage was apparent except the hinges had been torn from the firewall by the force. The windshield didn't get damaged nor the roof - the paint wasn't even scratched. The hood was too far damaged to close it and there was no way to hold it down for the duration of the trip. We removed it and tossed it into the ditch, hopefully the State Highway Department would haul it away.

An hour later, after Ron had calmed down and we all had a good chuckle about Ron's "new" car being damaged. Forty-five minutes later, all fourteen cars were once again hitting 65 per on the way to Oberlin's Museum rod run…and Ron's hoodless Caddy now looked like a hot rod…not the smooth kustom it's supposed to be!

Unbeknownst to Ron, several of his friends on the trip conspired on what should be done with the hood- they didn't want to leave it in the ditch. They ended up heading for home early on Sunday morn. Pat Friend had driven his '53 Chevy pick-up, so they stopped and picked up the hood and brought it back to Denver. In the months that followed, it was kept at a shop and those 14 people (and spouses/friends) that took that little trip each wrote a wry comment on it and signed the hood.

Ron put on an invitation only hot rod party in October of that year at his place and as a great surprise to him, we presented him with his 'old' hood at his party. Needless to say, he was quite surprised to see it, especially with all the names on it...it now hangs proudly in his garage.

Once back home and a week or so later, two hoods had been found and purchased, the hinges straightened and welded back on and within a year the whole car was stripped for a complete redo.

THE 'SHOULDA STAYED ON THE INTERSTATE' INCIDENT!

I like Good-guys' Scottsdale event...we've been several times cause we see cars we'll never see again. "Cars we'll never see again?" you ask? Yep, an example: Dan and I attended the 2009 WCK Santa Maria event...lots of nice cars...I asked several kustom car guys why they didn't come back to Kansas for the Leadsled Spectacular in July? Their answers: "No need to leave California, plenty of huge events right here." Hmmmmmmm, that may be, but I get tired of seeing the same cars at the same events...I need new "scenery." I assumed every car guy was like me...guess not.

Okay, I'm off my soapbox, not my forte! Many of you know me and my brother do several out-of-state events and rack up thousands of miles every summer. In July, 2013, we did a 4,552 mile loop in our '54 and '55 Cadillacs - Denver, CO, to Regina, Canada, followed 71 Canadian rodders to Good-guys Puyallup, Washington, event. Then Dan and I drove back east by ourselves to Yellowstone for their 43rd Annual rod run and then drove home.

But, this incident happened after the Scottsdale event. We were on our way home.

November 2006. Western New Mexico. Dan and I left Scottsdale Sunday – I'm driving the radical '57 Chevy, Dan's driving his '64 Super Sport. Highway 60 to Florence Junction, Route 79 south to Tucson, Arizona. Visited the Pima Air Museum and drove around the U.S. aircraft storage facilities...F-14's, Wart Hogs, B-52's, Apache helicopters, refueling tankers and many other kinds stored there. Monday morning, we took Interstate 10 east to Wilcox, AZ to see my long-time pal, Phil Roth. Arriving mid-morning, Phil showed us his 'collection' of cars and his'50 Buick fastback.

After lunch, we took I-10 east, figured we'd make Albuquerque by evening. Problem is, I'm not an Interstate lover, hate competing with eighteen wheelers and tourists taking pictures of me at 75 mph…most times waaaa-aaay too close to the sheet metal on my Chevy or Dan's and I must move over, slow and let them pass. After one "too-close-to-me-with-14-kids'-noses-pressed-to-the-van-windows-looking-at-me occasion, I'd had enough – I radioed Dan - "Find us a shortcut." He grabbed his Atlas, radioed back, "Lordsburg exit. North to Silver City, then east to Truth or Consequences… should make Albuquerque by nightfall."

Silver City is an old historic mining town, known for an 1895 flood…the town's streets ran north to south, built in the path of normal water runoff. Businesses sprang up, people dealt with the inconveniences of summer rain. The downtown area had high sidewalks to accommodate run-off. Meanwhile, uncontrolled grazing thinned plant life on the surrounding hills. During the night of July 21, a wall of water rushed downtown, digging a ditch in Main Street 55 feet lower than the original street level. Silver City's Main Street ended so businesses used their back doors as their entrances (Google is your friend!) from then on. Yes, that huge ditch is still there.

East of Silver City, we saw the Santa Rita open pit copper mine…watched big-as-houses trucks claw their way out of the pit hauling tons of copper laden material to the top. The pit was named for the old town, but you won't find it on any up-to-date map, it's gone. There was a Santa Rita - typical Southwestern mining community, kept its frontier flavor to the end. The town was first moved to satisfy the strip mine's ravenous Glory Hole, moved several times more until the hole was too large. The town disbanded in 1957 by a vote of city council. (Google is my friend!)

About 1:30, we had 90 miles to I-25, then north 150 miles to Albuquerque - piece of cake at 75 mph, but travel two-lanes, there's always something to see…New Mexico's Mimbres Mountains is gorgeous. The road started to narrow as we headed into the Gila National Forest…what we didn't know was the road was winding, curvy…and slow. Couldn't get close to 75 mph…20 mph into a right-hand uphill hairpin curve and 10 out to a left hairpin downhill and repeat, and repeat, for over three hours. With the four-speed in the rad '57, I never got into third the whole time and for Dan and his Powerglide, it was forever shifting up and down…at least there was no traffic. I'd built Nascar flares in the wheelwells of the '57...needless to say, I was shaving rubber off the sidewalls through every turn. We eventually reached Emory Pass, elevation 8178 feet. We could see the eastern New Mexico plains and a huge lake, probably 50 to 60 miles away (Elephant Butte Lake, 7 miles east of the city of Truth or Consequences). While parked at the viewpoint we heard an eighteen wheeler working its way up the mountain...we listened to it echo through the trees for half an hour before we decided daylight was going fast. It was 5 PM at that time and all downhill from the Pass... it took another half hour before we passed the upward eighteen wheeler...from there, we had the curvy highway to ourselves as the sun set behind the mountains...dusk darkened the eastern plains as we drove out of the tall pines and found a near straight highway downhill for 20 miles. By the time we got to I-25 it was 9 PM. We drove to Truth or Consequences knowing we'd never make Albuquerque...it'd taken us over eight hours to drive 90 miles!

In the morning, we decided on another shortcut- east around Albuquerque, hoping to get to Denver and home Tuesday evening - usually a seven hour Interstate drive from Albuquerque. As we left the motel, the gas gauge in the '57 read half a tank- figured 90-100 miles left. We'd fuel up in Bernardo, a town 89 miles north to our shortcut exit. Well, Bernardo wasn't...it was just a named exit... no gas station...uh-oh...!!! Highway 60 east took us to Mountainaire, 39 miles farther. I was running on fumes, I chugged to a stop 10 miles past the Interstate exit...but...we got smart over the years and carry a gallon of gas...two gallons should get me 35-40 miles. I pulled into the only station in Mountainaire and put 18 gallons of fuel into my 18 gallon tank...Dan took 17 gallons. Couldn't have gone much farther. With a full tank, we stayed on our New Mexico's eastern plains 'shortcut' and ended up catching I-25 south of Las Vegas, NM (yes, there is another town named Las Vegas...but no gambling there). From there it was another six hours home running 75 – 80 mph...

Yeah, maybe we shoulda stayed on the Interstate. Our "shortcuts" end up taking longer than normal, but the scenery is better than anything on any Interstate...our personal record for a "shortcut" is 75 miles in ten hours, along the Oregon coast...but this shortcut ranks a close second to that time spent sightseeing...and that's the main reason I prefer two-lanes...you'll never find Americana, its quirkiness or its gorgeous scenery on an Interstate...!!!

THE KANSAS INCIDENT

*Your best friend on a long road trip is a well-stocked tool box,
AND extra parts in the trunk!*

July, 2007. Beloit, Kansas. We'd left Good-guys Des Moines,
Iowa, event mid-afternoon Sunday, after viewing the award winners
and headed east. I didn't want to travel the Interstate between Des
Moines and Omaha again...I really hate that section of road-don't
know why, just do! I knew we'd have to spend the night somewhere
along the way simply because it was getting to the point that I don't
like driving at night anymore. I was in the radical '57 Chevy and Dan
was driving his '64 Impala SS. We'd stopped at some Iowa casino
and played some slots and they headed south. We crossed into
Missouri mid- afternoon and then as short time later we cruised into
St. Joe and crossed over into Kansas. We were making good time but
the day was getting shorter and the shadows were getting longer.
Figured we'd have to stop for the night soon. About 10 or fifteen
miles east of Beloit, Kansas, I was cruising along about to go under a
rail road track underpass when all of a suddenly the car simply died. I
radioed Dan that I was dead in the water and he pulled off.

It was still quite warm and the sun was hot as I coasted to the side
of the road and stopped the car in the shadow of the elevated rail road
tracks-gave me a bit of shade. I opened the hood to see what I could
see-and that was nothing! Everything was in place, I had plenty of
fuel and plenty of electricity for cranking the car over-it just wasn't
starting. Dan had backed up and was now questioning what had
happened.

"No fire,' I told him as I checked plug wires.

"Coil?" he asked.

"Maybe," I answered, "You got one with you?" I said
sarcastically, expecting a "No" answer. I was surprised when he
answered yes. He went to retrieve it and I got out a small wrench to
pull the nuts off the coil in the car. That's when I noticed it. The coil

wire had been pulled off by the accelerator…somehow, the coil wire was long enough that it wrapped itself around the accelerator linkage and when I stepped down on it to go up a small hill, the linkage grabbed hold of it and jerked it right off the coil and killed all the fire. Had Dan not had that coil he was going to replace the old one with, we might not have noticed the wire missing from the coil in our search to find out what happened and may have had to call a tow truck. Fortunately, between he and I we can deduce a problem in a short time. I replaced the end of it with a new 'ring', crimped it down and put it back on the coil and tightened the nut down. The car fired right up.

By this time, it was almost dark so we drove on into Beloit and got a motel room. We continued the rest of the way home on Monday. Moral of the story: If you can't fix your car on the side of the road, stay home. And that is something Dan or I have never done..!!!

THE HARD LUCK INCIDENT

Not such a great award to receive because it just means your car wasn't exactly ready for a long distance trip! The only thing you can blame it on is things break through no fault of your own. However, some people look forward to getting Hard Luck awards – not us!

June, 2009. Gering, Nebraska--We had heard about a great car show in Scottsbluff, Nebraska area so we decided to take a trip and participate in the festivities. I drove my Lavender 1955 Cadillac and Dan was in his Green flamed 1954 Caddy.

We departed the Denver area heading up 1-76 on the warm spring day for Fort Morgan. Getting off the Interstate, we turned north on a two-lane towards the Nebraska line and across the Pawnee Grasslands. Out on the prairie we stopped and watched the missiles fire out of the silos, (No, not really, but there are missile silos dotting the landscape and you can see them all along this route).

We gassed up in Kimball, Nebraska and ate lunch at a local cafe. The drive was only a four hour drive so we weren't in any big hurry. We arrived in Gering, a small "suburb" of Scottsbluff mid-afternoon. We found the host hotel and got checked in and registered for the car show. Talking to a few of the local rodders in the parking lot, we asked where the car wash would be. It was just a few blocks from the hotel, so as we were leaving the parking lot, Dan heard a pop in the rear of his car. We both stopped and got out to see what the noise was. While I stood next to the car, Dan drove ahead slowly. There was a cracking noise, sounded like the rear-end, especially from the left rear side. "Not much we can do about it now. Let's hope it doesn't get any more serious," I said.

Dan drove slowly to the car wash, listening to the clicking noise. The car wash was a good one and we got off all the bugs from the hood and grille. We headed back to the host hotel and talked to a few guys that directed us to a gentleman that worked on rear-ends out of his home garage. We drove the Caddy down to him, which wasn't far from the hotel, had him listen to it. We jacked up the rear and put the car in gear, but there was no noise from it. The guy had Dan stop the wheels from spinning and put it in neutral and wiggled the rear left tire. It was let off the jack stands and the guy deduced the rear-end had taken a dump.

"Oh great, now what do we do?" Dan asked. "Well, let's just enjoy the weekend and we'll figure out something in the meantime," I said. "That guy said we could still drive the car, but not any high speeds and he wouldn't attempt going back to Denver with it making that noise." We could drive in the parade on Saturday before the show in the park where the show and shine would be held.

Back at the hotel Dan and I discussed the problem and I thought the rear wheel bearings were the culprit cuz it wasn't making any noise when it was jacked up off the ground. So we called all the auto parts stores in the Scottsbluff area looking for rear wheel bearings for a 1954 Cadillac. Sure enough, we found some at the Advance Auto Parts store, but had to order them and they would be in early Saturday morning.

Saturday morning came early for us and we went over to Advance and picked up the bearings. We bought two figuring we might find someone local to press at least one on, but we never did after we asked a bunch of people about mechanics around there.

The parade was at nine o'clock, we got lined up and proceeded through the streets of Gering to the park. By the time we got to the park, it was already nearly filled with many vehicles that didn't drive in the parade. The park was nice lush green grass with a mild slope to it. We got parked and cleaned the cars up and went off walking, looking at the other fantastic machinery on the grounds. The morning went by fast and early afternoon we were approached by a reporter from the local paper that wanted to do a story on our Cadillacs. She asked a lot of questions and took pictures of both cars. We made the paper in the middle of the following week, the reporter sent Dan a copy in the mail. The show and shine was over at four, the banquet was held at six with awards following that. During the awards they called out the winners of the various classes and I won the "Best Custom" award. They called Dan's name for a "Sponsor's Award," which was Budweiser Beer. While Dan was up there, they also gave him the "Hard Luck" Award for the third member/bearings going out of his car. Along with that award was a One Hundred Dollar Bill! Yep, it went to good use!

After the awards, we asked one of club members if there was some place we could store the car on Sunday. We talked to George Leis and he said we could put it in his garage.

Sunday morning after breakfast we met George at his garage. His garage was at a used car dealership that we had driven by a couple of times while in Scottsbluff. We left Dan's Caddy there and drove my Caddy back to Denver.

Monday morning we hooked up Dan's twenty foot enclosed trailer to his '01 Chevy Silverado pickup and headed back to Scottsbluff to get his Cadillac. We arrived around noon, loaded the Caddy, had lunch with George, thanked him for the storage and headed back to Denver. We got back around six and put the Caddy in my back yard garage.

Later in that week we jacked up the car and pulled both axles out. The passenger's side was okay, but when the driver's came out so did the ball bearings. The keeper that holds the balls together had disintegrated and there were small pieces of metal in the housing that needed to be cleaned out.

Since we had new bearings we bought in Scottsbluff: our friend, Clint, took the axles and removed the old bearings and pressed on the new ones. Then Dan cleaned out the old grease from the axle housing. Clint reinstalled the axles, tightened everything up, put new fluid in the third member, installed the wheels and tires, and let it down off the jack stands. They've been in the car now for 8 years, will probably last another 8...or ten!

THE LIMON INCIDENT

This story is about the '55 Cadillac I'd built and its first "long distance" trip. The car took 5 ½ years to build from start to finish and this trip was the first highway trip I took with the new car!

JULY, 2011. Limon, ColoRODo. A little history first: It'd been 5 ½ years since I brought my '55 Cadillac home on a trailer from Lakewood, Colorado-a suburb of Denver. I'd purchased it as a failed project in April of 2005. Following the trailer was a 20 foot box trailer full of spare parts. We unloaded the '55 in my driveway and pushed it backward into my garage at the rear of my house. The box trailer was unloaded next and all the spare parts were set in the garage against the walls. The first thing my brother and I did was take inventory - I had nearly two of everything, and sometimes three of certain pieces, Almost enough to build two '55 Cadillacs, save a body and another frame.

Dan's '54 Cadillac had been running for a couple of years and we were slowly getting it looking good. We'd overhauled his stock 331" engine and Hydramatic transmission in 2009 and the car was running good. I'd been working on my '48 Cadillac Sedanet but wasn't getting much done with it when good friend Ron Brown drove up one afternoon in his new 1956 Cadillac two door hardtop. Seems an opportunity presented itself when he offered his 1937 Chevy street rod for sale-he got the running, driving Caddy and a 1955 Ford F-100 in exchange for his rod. Uh-oh, I'm the odd man out with my '48…and it doesn't look like it's going to get done anytime soon! So the '55 came available and I figured it'd only take me a year to get it on the road…boy, did I mis-guess on that one!

Sitting in the engine compartment of my "new" '55 Cadillac was a 1970 Cadillac 500 ci V8 engine. Yes, I said sitting simply because the motor mounts that had been used were way too tall and it put the engine way above the 1978 Pontiac Trans Am sub-frame that had been poorly installed. Besides that, between the motor mounts was a thick plastic block about 4 inches square and about 2 inches thick. Apparently the former owner was going to drill through the block and add a long bolt to hold the engine down. That was the first thing that would change. The hood was off the car and it was a good thing as the hood would probably never had gotten closed and latched. After we got the car unloaded and scoped out, I told my brother, Dan, that I could build this car in a year, two, tops...we'll see!

The former owner said the engine ran, had "good oil pressure" and the tranny was good, so I'd decided to put the car together enough to drive it for a while...do body work as I drove the car and the paint and interior would come along somewhere down the road. With the front clip off, I could scope out the way the engine sat on the "mounts" and I decided the engine needed lowering in the saddle. I removed the plastic pieces and that dropped the engine about two inches. The original Caddy mounts still had the engine setting too high so I literally tore the rubber off them and used just the metal. That lowered the engine another inch. Then I figured out why the engine was sitting so high –the external oil pump was now hitting the frame. Ooooooops! Now what? Back to the drawing board-time to rethink what I'd just done – it wasn't going to work that way. I thought about it for a while and called up some friends - they told me a remote oil pump would work so I called the guys at On-Track Racing Supply and ordered up the necessary parts. I mounted the remote on the underside of the grille pan and hooked everything up.

After that, my brother and I removed the body from the frame. That was a whole adventure in itself. We used two floor jacks-at the front together then moved them to the rear. We started by jacking up the front firewall brace. When we got it high enough we slipped a four by four wooden beam across the entire front of the body - did the same at the rear and then we raised it high enough to get a concrete block under the wooden brace. We'd set it on 8 inch tall concrete blocks and moved the floor jacks to the front to do the same thing. Back and forth we went-raising the car 8 inches at time until we got it where we wanted. It took us a few hours to get the body high enough to slide the chassis out from under the body - the front was easy since the car had no front fenders on it but the body at the rear had to go higher to clear the frame that kicked up in the rear over the rear end. Needless to say, the body was five feet off the floor and the roof was just a few inches from the ceiling of the garage by that time and stacked on plenty of concrete blocks.

The body sat like that for several months. I got under it, cleaned the bottom and sprayed it with Lizardskin. The car had been a Colorado car all its life so it was virtually rust-free. After I got done with the bottom of the car, I concentrated on the chassis. The sub-frame had been attached crudely and it had been Mig wire welded...and not very well. There were holes blown through the metal and chicken-shit piles of welds all over it. I knew that wasn't going to hold together very well, or very long for all the highway trips I had planned for the car so I cleaned it all up and ground off all the chicken-shit welds and built some fish-plates out of 1/8" steel plate. When I was satisfied with the fish plating, I borrowed a trailer, loaded up the chassis and hauled it to Quentin Sonnenfeld - a local street rod builder. Quentin Tig-welded the fish plating on and welded up some of the other factory holes that were no longer needed.

Back home, I painted the frame gloss black and moved it back under the Cadillac body. I found all the rubber pads that fit on the frame's body mounts and the long bolts. It took about as long to let the body back down as we removed a pair of blocks from the rear and then moved the jacks to the front to remove a pair. When we got close, I got out the tape measure to see if we were setting the body down perfectly. We were close-we did have to juggle the chassis a bit to equal out the distance on both sides but it wasn't that hard.

In early 2008, the front clip was put back on the chassis and I proceeded to wire the car. I put in a tilt column and worked on getting the column shifter working. I was close enough to driving that I set a goal: the First of May for the Stray Kat event in Bartlesville, Oklahoma. I still had a radiator to put in, some work on the dash to do, a new grille pan to build and a few other things. The stock green interior was put back in - it wasn't all torn up or worn out so it'd be OK for a while.

Well, the Stray Kat rod run goal was missed, things just didn't work out as planned cuz the Caddy brakes didn't cooperate. In early

June 2008, I was able to drive the car for the first time after I got exhaust under it. It'd been three years since I rolled the Cad into my garage - so much for my "I'll knock it out in a year!"

Over the course of the next year, I got the body whipped into shape and in primer, the dash got finished, the grille got built, the fender skirts got built and a few miles got put on the car by going to some local rod runs. The engine was definitely needing a rebuild, it burned lots of oil regardless of the fact that it ran good.

In early 2009, I had the interior done, thinking I was just a few months away from a paint job. In July, me, Dan and our good friend Ron Brown drove our Cadillacs to Salina. None of our cars were finished and at the time were simply works in progress. We had a good time and we had a couple people tell us that "it's awesome to see those three Caddys rolling into an event."

In September, my brother and I drove our Caddy's to Wichita for the Starliner event...which was a mistake on my part. I shouldn't have taken the '55 Caddy...ya see, it took six quarts of oil to get to Salina in July (and another six home). In August, I didn't go to the HAMB drags in Joplin cuz I didn't trust the engine in the car to make the 13 hour trip...and so, in September, the engine was running fine, it was getting decent gas mileage, I figured OK, one more trip with the Caddy to the Starliner event in Wichita before I tear it down...should have listened to my gut and took one of my other cars...but the Caddy is so much fun to drive. Well, it took 8 quarts of oil to get to Wichita...and 12 to get home to Denver...time to rebuild the engine!

Between October, and December of 2009, the front clip got pulled, then the new interior came out as well as the glass...then the doors and trunk came off...and the engine came out and went to the rebuilder. The firewall got painted body color as well as the inner fenders and under the hood. The front fenders got some Raptor undercoating.

The new engine showed up on Saturday, December 12. For the next few months, the car got put back together and scheduled in at the body shop. The new engine was fired in late February and sounded good. In March, the car was taken to good friend Len Hoogland, the body man, and a new goal of Salina's KKOA event late July looks promising.

On May 20th, Len called and said the car was ready for paint. It looked good and I drove it home from his body shop. Len scheduled the paint for early June - won't leave me but a month or so to put the car back together and make Salina. No matter, may not make that goal either. I'd missed the Cad's debut at Mick Bryant's SK500 in Dewey, OK, in May. I missed its debut at the ColoRODo Good-guys event in June. I'd missed the debut at the NSRA event in Pueblo, ColoRODo. Hopefully, this goal will stick as I was close to getting the car done.

The car was painted in two-tones of purple and sprayed with 3 coats of clear. The body work Len had done was magnificent - the car was straight and flat. Couldn't wait to get it back together, drive it and show it off.

After completely busting my ass for weeks putting the Caddy back together, and really looking forward to the Salina KKOA 30th Anniversary event, I can definitely say that excrement occurs (or for those of you that prefer plainer English -- "shit happens,") and I can feel right about saying it.

There are thousands and thousands of actions that take place in the assembly of a car, and as many parts. You can do the best you can to control each of the actions that you have some semblance of control over. However, try as you may, not every one of those actions will be absolutely perfect.

Unfortunately, it just takes just one of those uncounted thousands of actions to stop you dead in your tracks. Besides, when you do most of the work yourself, those uncounted thousands of items can sometimes go awry. It's not like I planned a failure, I built this car from a dog that rightly should have been placed in a junkyard and even though it took five years, the planning, and work, wasn't shoddy at all.

Worse part of any build is that our mutual friend, Murphy, could rear his ugly head at the first chance he was given. Well, this time that gremlin named Murphy was way out of my control (and maybe my engine builder's as well). I didn't make it to Salina.

At Midnight Wednesday I was done. Done putting the car back together, needless to say, I was exhausted cuz I hate the last minute thrash, it takes way too much to get it done and most times, things don't always go right so you have to do them twice or three times to make it look good or work like it's supposed to. We'd been working on the Cad for weeks after I got the car painted, putting in the grille and park lights, wiring everything, adding front inner fender panels, securing side and hood trim, interior windshield moldings, gauges, glove compartment door and box, CB radio, under dash panel to hold the A/C vents, hanging the doors and adjusting them, putting on the roof scoops, glueing down the package tray upholstery, mounting the rear back rest and lower cushion after we put in the rear arm rests, attaching the door panels, door moldings, door handles and cranks, adding the faux wood grain to the dash, new bulbs in the dash and interior lights, building an in-dash mount for the stereo, and cover, putting the top of the dash back on, cleaning the new windshield and windows, balancing/mounting white wall tires, slapping hubcaps on and the very last thing I did was to attach the fender skirts to the Caddy. I was ready and tired and yet, looking forward to the 7 hour trip to Salina the next morning.

Anyway, after a short 5 hour "nap"- I rolled out of bed slowly Thursday morn. Go time was 6 AM. I fired up the Caddy and backed it out of the garage. My bro showed up at 5:45 and we headed for the gas station. We left Denver just about on time, heading east and looking forward to the drive. There were four of us in our little caravan, I was the last car in line cuz I like it that way. I like to look around a lot and being last in line, I don't have to worry much about what's in front of me and I can hold an even speed. Since the engine was new and only had 100 miles on it, I varied the speed in an effort to break it in properly, at the same time, I didn't turn on the stereo cuz I wanted to listen to the engine, make sure it wasn't going to do anything strange. All the time my bro is calling me on the CB. "You OK back there?" I was OK, but something gnawed at my gut, something didn't feel right, felt like something bad was going to happen on this trip. I pushed it deeper into the back of my mind. I quietly hoped it wasn't.

Ten miles passed easily. Then twenty miles came and went without a hitch. Thirty-five and the engine seemed to like the highway. Fifty miles from home, the car was running strong, sounding good and handling very well. I was beginning to get a bit more comfortable. The chatter on the CB picked up a bit more, our first stop, Limon, 80 miles from home was only 30 miles away at that point, we were to meet the ColoRODo Springs Lonely Knights there and run into Salina with them.

Seventy miles into the journey I was stoked, the engine sounded good and was strong, now I almost had 200 miles on the engine. I felt it was going to be a good run.

Then I heard it!!!!

Sounded like a lifter rattling just a bit, I really didn't want to hear it...but I didn't have any tunege to turn down and the CB wasn't chattering. I listened a bit more, figured it might be OK if I'd give it a minute. Not happening! Not going away! I let off the accelerator hoping it was a lifter and it would pump back up, gave it a minute and pressed down on the accelerator. I glanced down at my oil pressure gauge. It'd been running a solid 50 pounds of pressure and all of a sudden it dropped to forty. I didn't like the look of that. I let off again, nothing changed so I stepped down again. That's when I heard it, a low rattling knock in the bottom of the engine. I called my bro on the CB, told him to roll his window down cuz I was coming up alongside him. Asked him to listen as I let off the gas and stepped down. I could tell by the look on his face that the sound coming from the engine wasn't good, he shook his head, that ain't good at all. We pulled off to the side of the highway and opened the hood. I shut it off and started it up and it sounded like the whole bottom of the engine was coming loose. The trip to Salina just got cancelled.

I nursed the car the four remaining miles into Limon at about 20-30 mph. Good thing there weren't any CHP around. Right about the time we got there, the Springs bunch was pulling in so I explained what happened. Dan and I discussed my options - twenty miles to the south lived a friend, we could park the car on his drive, IF we could get it there, it'd be safe til we got back (three hours killed and/ or completely destroying the engine on the way there), or, my bro and I could take his Caddy and go back to Denver, get his truck and trailer, drive back to Limon load the Caddy and take it home (four to five hours killed but the engine would be saved), or, call my good friend Ron Brown to see how busy he was. The last option sounded best and I could ride back to Denver with him, park the Caddy in my garage and drive my '40 Studey to Salina. Problem with that, it'd kill the whole day and I didn't want to hold up our other companions all day. I called Ron and it took a few phone calls back and forth before we got the rescue sorted out. My friend Ron Brown, has never let me down when I'm stuck somewhere. He postponed a sprinkler install job he had scheduled, called me back and told me he'd be there in an hour. Once he got to Limon, it took 20 minutes to load the Caddy cuz it's so low (I have no air bags on the car), and we had to remove the skirts to get it into his box trailer. Ron asked me if I'd like to take his truck and trailer and haul the car to Salina, unload it in the park and let everyone, at least, see it. I declined. I'm not a trailer person, I'm a driver. If the car wouldn't, or couldn't, get there under its own power, it'd stay home. Besides, the Caddy is not a show car, it's a driver and if I took it there, I'd want to drive it around, show it off. Not happening!!!

In the meantime, I'd decided I didn't want to drive my other car, I was bummed. Dan suggested we toss my stuff into his Caddy's trunk and we could STILL go to Salina. No sense not attending the party just because I didn't have a car to drive. Ron understood that and suggested he'd take my Cad to his place, leave it in the trailer and I could pick it up when I got back and he'd still have time to do his scheduled sprinkler job. For the second time, Ron came and rescued me. Two hours later Ron headed west, Dan and I headed east for Salina.

Disappointed??? Saddened??? Sure, but what could I do??? There are very few things that make me angry and this was something I could do nothing about so no sense making everyone around me miserable with some mean-spirited words, or display of wrench-throwing emotion (I don't do that anyway). It happens! Murphy is always hanging around somewhere near, but as I was telling friends in Salina, shit happens for a reason. Could be my guardian angel knew something I didn't and prevented me from making the rest of the trip, she was simply watching over me, or the good Lord just made the rest of my life a whole lot easier and if that's the case, my prayers for my safe trip had just been answered and I hoped my guardian angel would ride with us on the rest of the trip. Regardless, at this point, I'll never know but I am positive she rides with us all the time.

We had a good time in Salina, we had a safe trip, including a great time talking with old friends and we met some great new people and Dan's '54 Caddy, our sled for the weekend, got a lot of looks and averaged 18.7 miles per gallon over the whole 1000 mile round trip and that's not bad for a 56 year old car. And, as someone at Salina told me: "Now you have bragging rights." I'm not convinced destroying a new engine was something to "brag" about...!!!

I called the engine builder when we got back home and he came over to diagnose the problem. The engine was pulled and rebuilt, the blame fell on the remote oil unit. Spun bearings on the both the crank and the rods. To alleviate that problem from happening again, I removed the motor mounts I'd made and redid them. I raised the engine approximately 1 ½ inches - just enough to put the stock external oil pump back on the block. I removed the remote oil unit and bought a "blue-printed" Cadillac oil pump. That solved the whole oiling problem. By late summer the car was back together.

In the years since, the engine has never missed a lick and some of the stories you've read and will read here have involved the Cadillac. Many miles have been put on my Cadillac and Dan's and many more are planned.

Just so you know, Dan and I like to have a project in the winter months, in the last four years, Dan and I have put together a 1960 Pontiac station wagon and sold it (went to Detroit, Michigan), a 1960 Chevy Brookwood station wagon and sold it (went to St. Paul and then to Wisconsin), a 1952 Willys gasser and sold it (went to Marion, Ohio) and we've just completed a 1963 Chevy Super Sport and sold it. Now it's time to get after and really finish the '48 Cadillac I have owned for over 19 years. Hopefully it'll be on the road by Summer of 2018!

THE RANCH INCIDENT

Two years after I'd gotten my '55 Cadillac street worthy and having won several awards at several different rod runs, I finally won a big award –the one thing that would tell me I'd hit a home run with the way I built my Cadillac.

September, 2012. Loveland, ColoRODo. I won the "Traditional Homebuilt" award at the Good-guys show at the Ranch in Loveland with my '55 Cadillac!

Saturday morning was the morning GG's has their special sections-sometimes there are different events with different cars but this time it was the Traditional Homebuilt, for cars that were built traditionally-meaning whitewalls, fender skirts, old hot rods, Oldsmobile engines in older rods, and the like. No modern stuff-no billet, no super large wheels and rubber band tires-old school, traditional...

My Cadillac still looked good after two years of highway driving and going rod running and it was polished up and cleaned up, even emptied the trunk of the usual stuff I carry. Of course in order for the judges to see the whole car, the hood had to be open, the doors had to be open and the trunk opened. It was almost like an indoor car show outside.

I parked the Caddy in that section, open from10am to 3pm. Dan and I cruised around in his Cadillac, or walked the vendor exhibition area or just looked at cars. We seldom sit by our cars unless we're having a break or eating lunch. We like to look at other cars-can't understand why people go to a car show and sit behind their cars all day! Anyway, when we finally went back to the car after 3pm, I was shocked to find the yellow piece of paper stating that I had won. I was to be in the Winner's Circle by 10 am the next morning and drive the car through the awards ceremony at 2pm. I was elated. I drove home that night congratulating myself for the win.

Sunday morning, we drove back up to Loveland. As we pulled through the gate, the Cadillac started missing. What the hell? What's up with this misfiring? I slipped the car into neutral and revved it up, black smoke poured from the tailpipes. Oh great, just what I need today! My big day and my Caddy ain't having any of it! Fortunately, just past the entrance the cruising road goes downhill. If I can get over the hump, I'll coast into the winner's circle. By the time I got there, the car wasn't blowing black smoke any longer but it was still missing. The GG's officials directed me to the "Winner's Circle and I had had to be there in time to get the Caddy parked in about the middle of all the other winners. I managed to get the car parked and opened the hood, trying to figure out why it was missing. Why now? I've been driving the Caddy for two years and never had a problem with the carb...why now?

As I was standing there scratching my head, good friends Len Hoogland and Bob Kenworthy came by to congratulate me. I asked Len if he knew anything about original Quadrajet four barrel carbs. He asked why I was asking, told him of the problem I was having. The worse part of sitting in the winner's circle is everyone in the world came over to see the winners and here I am with the hood open trying to figure out why my Caddy won't run. The exact wrong place for the car to act up. Len, being a master mechanic and bodyman suggested he take a look at it so we pulled the air cleaner off. We talked about what it was doing and he thought maybe the floats were stuck. He asked if I carried a tool box, which I always do so I got it out. He said we'd overhaul the carb right there if we need to. Friend Bob said he'd help so both took the top off the carb. Just so you know, I have no idea how to rebuild a carb but I was getting an education right there in the winner's circle.

Needless to say, it took some doing on Len's part to get the carb working without blowing black smoke. The carb would idle for a few minutes then die. He deduced the power valve was bad. Bob asked if finding another carb would help? Could we take the valve out of that and put it in my carb? Len said that'd work but where were we going to get another carb? Bob said he remembered seeing a couple in the swap meet. He'd go check to see if the guy was still there. He came back with two used Quadrajet four barrels and he and Len proceeded to tear them apart. By that time, we had tools all over the ground in front of the car, dirty paper towels stuffed down in the grille so they wouldn't blow around and about 20 people standing around the front of the car trying to figure out what was happening.

The time was flying by, about noon we still didn't have the car running correctly-it would run if I kept my foot into it some but it wouldn't idle on its own. I had visions of me not driving through the awards ceremony and at a Good-guys event, IF the car doesn't drive through the ceremony on its own, it won't get an award. My big chance to drive through the ceremony and get my big award was beginning to fade! About 1:30, after tearing the carb apart for the 54th time and putting it back together the same amount, Len announced it was the best he could do to get me through the awards. He told me to fire the car up for the last time and he'd adjust the mixture. He said it'd get me home but since it wouldn't idle, he wasn't sure it'd make it through the ceremony. I fired up the car and while he adjusted the carb. Just as he was about done, it died again. He asked me if I had an electric fuel pump on the car, I said I did. He said that might be the problem-it's forcing too much fuel into the carb and it's dying because of it. He said start it up and let it idle but when it starts to die, turn off the pump (I'd wired the pump to a separate switch and not to the ignition-that way I could turn it off and on when I wanted). I did as he asked and the carb idled fine. I turned the pump back on just before the carb ran out of gas and turned it off again just a second later. I did that several times while the car idled fine. Len said, "That might be the only way you'll get through the awards." I said I could handle that...and that's how I drove through the awards. It was kinda tuff to accept the plaque with my right hand while turning the fuel pump off and one while the car idled, but I did it. Once I had the award, I put the car in gear and drove away.

While this incident isn't exactly "fixing it on the side of the road"...and it wasn't exactly ME doing the fixing, I was there observing and handing wrenches and screwdrivers and getting a carburetor lesson, it did, nonetheless, get fixed away from home.

Could I do something like that again? I doubt it, but I'd bet I could find someone that could.

If it wasn't for good friends Len Hoogland and Bob Kenworthy coming to my rescue that morning, I wouldn't have that plaque hanging on my wall...and I wouldn't have won the Nationwide Traditional Homebuilt award that happened later in the year. Since I had won at one of the GG's events, I was placed in another contest-a nationwide contest of 16 winners of the Traditional Homebuilt. I won that one, too, and got a $500.00 gift card from Speedway, sponsor of the event, a very nice Speedway Jacket and another plaque to hang on my wall.

I drove the car home the same way that afternoon, turning on and off the fuel pump for 60 miles. Shortly after that, I used part of that $500.00 gift card and ordered a new Edelbrock carb from Speedway and put in on the Caddy. It's still on there yet today and still runs very good. Thanx Speedway! I'd be remiss if I didn't say a huge THANX to Len Hoogland and Bob Kenworthy.

While this story isn't exactly "fixing your car on the side of the road" and it wasn't exactly ME fixing the car, it did get fixed away from home and my garage.

THE STRAY KAT INCIDENT

Dan and I had been driving our Cadillacs to most of the local rod runs and cruises but we hadn't had them on a long distance trip since I'd won at Good-guy's. We'd been to the Stray Kat 500 previously but not with our "finished" Cadillacs so we decided to head down there again.

May, 2014. Goodland, Kansas. The morning we left at 7AM, it was cold…of course, this was May, and in ColoRODo May is almost as bad as April and March for snowstorms. Sometimes it doesn't warm up til June around Denver! Well, we'd just had a snowstorm the day before we were to leave. During the snow, both Dan and I questioned our sanity on leaving since we knew the roads wouldn't even be cleared yet and we wondered if the storm was headed to Kansas –the exact direction we were going. Fortunately, in ColoRODo, in early Spring, the snow doesn't stick around long-it melts rather quickly. Regardless, it's a 12-13 hour drive to Dewey, Oklahoma from our home and hate to say it, to save time and drive on cleared roads - it's Interstate most of the way.

I was driving my '55 Cadillac and following Dan in his '54 Cadillac. To add to the regrets about this trip was the fact there neither of us had heaters or defrosters in our cars. When we left at 7AM it was about 35 degrees and both of us wore sweatshirts, heavy coats, stocking caps and gloves. Fortunately, there were clear (patches of wet and dry) pavement until we got close to Limon, ColoRODo, about 90 miles from home. The roadway got worse and worse around there until we were running on a pair of tracks down the middle of the Interstate. The white lines were literally slush covered and we couldn't tell there where the two-lanes of traffic were. Good thing there weren't any 18 wheelers trying to get around us! In Limon, they close I-70 in bad weather so all the trucks stay in a couple of truck stops there. We rolled through just after they opened the highway. Past Limon, it got worse until we were chugging along at about 45 mph in heavy slush and some light snow – knew right then we weren't going to make the trip in 12 hours!

It took a while but eventually we drove out of the snow and the highway became drier-speed went up, so did the temperatures and the sun came out. No problems now...should be back on our original 12 hour trip again...or so we thought! There are 75 miles between Limon and Burlington, which is just this side of the Kansas border. My Cadillac doesn't do well on fuel –usually gets about 13-15 mpg and I'd filled up in Denver just before we got on the Interstate, can usually get 200 miles out of a tank. Near Burlington, my Cadillac started coughing-felt like it was out of fuel although the gauge said I still had about half a tank. I radioed Dan and told him of my problem and asked if he knew where the nearest gas station was.

"Burlington," was the answer. I didn't make Burlington. About 7 miles out the coughing and jerking got worse and I saw an off-ramp. "Take it Dan, I'm getting off," I radioed.. "I think I'm out of gas!" I hate parking alongside the Interstate so I always try to get off it. As I'm coasting to the top of the off-ramp, the car starts running again. "What the hell?" My gas gauge reads half a tank.

"Does this road go into Burlington" I asked Dan. He answered, "it does about a mile to the north-sort of a frontage road."

"Let's go into Burlington and I'll get some gas," I said, "If I can make it that far!"

It took us about ten minutes to get into town. I bought some Premium just to pep up the engine a bit (I usually just run Unleaded Regular). After I gassed up, the car seemed to run fine - I revved it up a few times and nothing -no jerking or coughing, so through downtown to catch the Interstate again.

Down the on-ramp and up to speed in just a few seconds-car runs good! I'm out front now as Dan said he'd follow to see if I was leaking any fuel. Okay, no more problems please! Thirteen miles past Burlington we cross into Kansas and guess what? Road construction. West-bound lanes were moved to the east bound part of the Interstate. One lane traffic for the next 20 miles. Just what we need, glad the car is running good now. Yep - -Cough! Jerk! Cough! Awww Damn. Not now! Yep, NOW!!!

Worse part, I now have Dan behind me and he has an eighteen wheeler behind him and ten to fifteen cars behind the truck. Even though the speed "limit" through the construction is 55 – me- going only 40 was holding up traffic and people were getting real impatient. My Cadillac is coughing and jerking like it's running out of gas. Can't be, I've got a full tank. I radioed Dan, "I've got to get off this Interstate, but where?" There were no shoulders or pull-outs in the construction area and no off-ramps immediately ahead. "Find something," Dan says. "The eighteen wheeler is honking his damned horn at me!" No more than he says that and I see an old closed cross-over just ahead on the right side. I say "Right here" and hit my brakes to quickly turn into it. I literally slide into it and it is muddy and wet, pull into it as far as I can get to allow Dan in. By this time, traffic behind us is at a stop and I'm thinking they're wondering what the hell we're doing and are saying to themselves "Damned old cars on the highway!" The eighteen-wheeler is honking his horn so much I swear the air horns are going to vibrate off the top of the cab! Relax pal, you can't be in that big a hurry!

It took a few minutes for all the traffic to pass while we sat there. Dan radios the usual question, "What are we going to do now?" One of his favorite questions every time something goes wrong!

"I really don't know what's wrong with the car," I answer. "It runs but it doesn't. Don't know what's wrong with it. Think we'd best go back to Burlington and see if we can figure out why it's acting this way, if we can get back there." It took a few minutes until we had a clear shot in both directions to pull out onto the highway and head back west. I'm sure both Dan and I knocked down a couple of the center stripe cones getting out of that muddy hole we were in. Mud flew off the tires as we headed west and in a few minutes we were back in Burlington, but it wasn't smooth. The Cadillac jerked and coughed the whole way.

I stopped at an auto parts place and opened the hood. The first thing I checked was the in-line fuel filter. Clear. The carb filter was next. Nope, not it! The carb was squirting gasoline into the carb just fine, too. We deduced it wasn't electrical and the coil in the HEI was new just before this trip. I was at a loss. After some discussion and spending about 45 minutes trying to figure the cause, we decided the trip was off and we'd just as well try to go back home-some 165 miles away. "Will the car make it that far?" Dan asked.

"I sure don't know, but it beats sitting here cuz I can't find anything wrong."

"OK, let's take that two- lane we came in on..." Dan said, "stay off the interstate for now."

As I headed west out of town, I was moving about 45 mph, the car seemed to run good. But when I kicked the speed up to 55, or more, the coughing and jerking started again. I did this several times trying to figure out why a higher speed would cause those problems - eventually figured it had to be crud in the carb (again!). Okay, guess we'll drive home at 45 mph if we can't go faster! Will make a long trip but if we get the car home without having to hire a flatbed we'll be doing good.

It was 4:00 in the afternoon when I finally pulled into my garage. I put the Caddy in the garage and closed the door, called a couple of friends to get their opinion on why the car ran that way. Of course, I got varying opinions, none of which helped me until later that night as I was watching television. It hit me right in the forehead – I originally had an electric fuel pump on the car and I'd unhooked it when I put a manual fuel pump back on the engine. I'd installed a second filter in place of the electric fuel pump at the rear of the car. Maybe that filter was clogged.

The next morning I jacked the car up, slipped a jack-stand under the frame and took off the fender skirt. I'd mounted the pump in the wheel-well so I could get at it easier than having to crawl under the car every time I wanted to change the pump or the filter. I removed the filter and cut it open (I used an aluminum filter instead of one of those plastic filters). Inside was brown plastic-like pieces, looking like a plastic type grocery bag. Did someone shove a bag down into the fill tube and it eventually made its way to the tank and clogged up the line? Really perplexed me. Why would someone do that to me? I realized that not everyone likes me and maybe at some show I pissed someone off and they'd shoved the bag in to get "even" when I wasn't looking and the bag eventually came apart down in the tank. I took the fuel line off the carb and took an air hose and blew the line forward out...nothing came out so figured the filter stopped it all and in the process stopped the flow of fuel to the carb, especially at a higher speed than 45. That was slow enough to let some fuel through the garbage but faster it piled more up in the filter! It was then I realized that I was going to have to pull the gas tank to have it cleaned out. Just about the same time I realized that - wait a minnit, I'd had that tank cleaned and coated 6 or 7 years ago, when I was first building the car...one of the very first things I did.

When I got the tank out-sure enough, pieces of that coating came out with the fuel when I dumped it out and I was going to have to have someone clean the tank really good. I found a guy that said he could do it and yep, he did, except it took him a month to get all the old coating out by heating and scraping. He told me he found a better coating, one that wouldn't be affected by Unleaded Regular and it ended up costing me $300 total. Best part: ever since then, the car has run beautifully although my gas mileage has not improved a bit. Worse part: could have purchased a new tank for less than what I spent having it cleaned, but like anything else, when it comes to cars and building them and driving them - ya live and learn!

THE IDAHO INCIDENT

It took the radiator business nearly three months for the Cadillac's gas tank to get cleaned out and resealed. Still don't know why! I had been itching to get the Caddy back on the road as we'd planned many months ago to go to take a looo-oooo-nnnn-ggg cruise to Canada. With about a month to spare, I got the tank back in the '55 Caddy and for the second time in as many years, Dan and I were off on another trip to Canada to meet up with our good Canadian friends we had met just a year previous.

August, 2014. Hayden, Idaho. Before I get into this story, I'd just like to recap our first trip to Canada in 2013. That trip racked up over 5,000 miles in two weeks, was a trouble-free trip and we had a great time! So, here's the recap: *In 2013, Dan and I cruised our two Cadillacs up to Regina, Saskatchewan, to enjoy the "Western Canada Power Cruise". It took us three days to drive from Denver, ColoRODo to Regina, and we arrived there on a Monday evening. Let me tell you, is it ever flat in that part of Canada!*

After an over-night stay in Regina, the 71-car tour group headed west towards Medicine Hat, Alberta, on Trans-Canada Highway One, for our second over-night stay. Basically it was an un-eventful five-hour drive. While in the city, there was a Tuesday night cruise at the Target store's parking lot near the motel, the entire tour participated

Wednesday morn, the tour left early for a long day of traveling. Our first stop was Calgary for lunch and then from there, it was westward through Banff National Park with a side trip to beautiful Lake Louise. The lake was a pretty Emerald Green fed by glaciers from the nearby mountains. We had an over-night stay in Golden, British Columbia, in the high Canadian Rockies. Thursday morning we drove west and south to Merritt, B.C., our last "official" over-night on the tour, but still in the beautiful Canadian Rockies. That evening we gave away some door prizes to the participants on the WCPC and our "Coolest Cruiser" Award to one of the members.

Afterwards, we lounged around talking about the tour with Chris McMillan, the man that organized this one. The sun finally set about 11 PM so we retired for the night, as we wanted to get an early start for tomorrow and the last leg of our trip to Puyallup, Washington and the Good-Guy's event.

We departed Merritt Friday morning, heading south through Hope, Chilliwack and into the U.S. of A. at Sumas, Washington. We caught I-5 at Bellingham and drove south through Seattle and on south to Puyallup for the Good-guys Pacific Northwest Nationals at the Western Washington State Fair-grounds. It was a fun three days of cruising and showing off our Cadillacs, visiting with old and new friends and looking at all the nice vehicles on the grounds. We decided that we would come back to this show again, sometime in the future and since the previous Canada trip was trouble-free, why not do it again?

In August, 2014, Chris McMillan had again arranged another tour, this time to Spokane, Washington, which was almost the next best thing to Puyallup. Dan and I again drove our Cadillacs up to Medicine Hat, Alberta, and met up with the Canadian guys. When we left Medicine Hat, we took a more southern route across the lower part of Alberta and British Columbia Provinces. We had one over-night stay in Cranbrook B.C. then down to Spokane, Washington, for the Good-guys Great Northwest Nationals.

Those three days of fun went by way too fast and we departed Spokane on Sunday afternoon and headed east to Post Falls, Idaho, to see a friend that had a street rod shop and was building some nice stuff. After visiting with him and viewing his projects, we went to Coeur D'Alene and drove around the lake like we were tourists, which we were!

From there we headed north to Hayden as we'd heard about a cruise night that evening. On the drive up, Dan's car started to run rough so we found a motel and got checked in. We got there mid-afternoon and had time so we decided to check the wires and plugs to figure out the problem. I pulled off the coil wire and the top of the distributor cap literally crumble in my hand. Well, that's certainly part of the problem! Just down the street from the motel was a NAPA

167

store so I walked down and bought new points, rotor and distributor cap. Once all that was installed, Dan took the car out for a test run and it was running like new. Problem solved! Not quite!

We did make it to the cruise night and the next morning we headed out for Sand Point, Idaho, but about ten miles on the road Dan's Cadillac started to act up again. We pulled off onto a dirt road and opened the hood to figure out if the points had closed on us. An older gentleman rode up on his bicycle and asked if we needed help and we told him our problem. He said he had a shop and we were welcome to use it for our repairs, best part was he was only a half a block from where we were. We managed to get the car started and drove down to his garage. This time the points were OK so we figured it was the fuel system not getting enough fuel to the carburetor. After some discussion amongst us, I drove to Athol, a small town down the road that had a parts store, to get the needed parts while Dan waited. We bought some new rubber hose and an electric fuel pump to deliver the fuel. When I returned, the car was up in the air and I crawled under the car and installed the pump and ran a wire to the front of the car and installed a switch. That seemed to solve the problem, but unfortunately, that was not the end of this incident.

Our intended destination for the night was Kalispell, Montana, and we were doing great on the way simply because there was a lot of beautiful scenery in that part of the country. As we neared Kalispell, Dan's Caddy started to act up again. Problem was, it wasn't getting enough fuel to the carb as it would idle fine, but when it was given more power it would choke and sputter. Just outside of Kalispell, we again pulled off the road to try to figure out the problem. We were just off the entrance to a housing development and a lady in a new Cadillac stopped. She asked us if we were having problems and said her husband was a retired mechanic and could probably help figure out the problem. His shop was just a few miles back up the road if we could get there. it. She called him and told him we were on our way. When we got there and explained our problem, he said bring it into the shop and put it up on his lift. We found the problem right away. The new rubber fuel line that had been installed was being smashed between the axle and the frame – I hadn't routed it well enough because I had to lay on my back and work with a flashlight at the other garage. I was able to reroute the line so that there was plenty of room between the axle and the frame. That solved the fuel starvation problem.

We eventually got to Kalispell late afternoon and stayed in Kalispell the whole next day, visited and drove around Flathead Lake and then made our way up through Glacier National Park and over Logan Pass on the "Run to the Sun" highway. It was cloudy and rainy and we didn't get to see much of the pass so on the other side we headed up to Cardston, Alberta, Canada, to stay there for two days while we attended a car show in Waterton Lakes National Park on Sunday. Both Dan and I won the Long Distance award there.

On Monday morning, after leaving Canada for our trip home, we again went through Glacier National Park and over Logan Pass. The weather had cleared and what a beautiful sight it was to see the mountains from there. We drove through Yellowstone, past the Tetons and into Jackson, Wyoming, and crossed into ColoRODo south of Laramie. Dan's '54 Cadillac ran fine the rest of the way home and had no other problems. When we got home, we cleaned the carb, replaced the fuel filters and left the electric fuel pump in the car and it's used occasionally.

THE HALL OF FAME INCIDENT

Dan and I took one car on this trip - my '55 Cadillac. This was a group tour of 50 cars leaving from the Good-guys event at Loveland, ColoRODo, to Bowling Green, Kentucky for the Good-guys event there. After we got home from this tour, I wrote Marc Meadors (President of Good-guys) to tell him I wouldn't do another tour with them. The reason: absolutely no one wanted to stay together on the 1500 mile trip...it seemed it was simply a race to the next stop. Not my idea of a "road tour"!

September, 2015. Conway, Arkansas. The advertising in the Good-guys magazine said "Travel with us and your friends on the way to Bowling Green, Kentucky from the Ranch in Loveland, ColoRODo" or something like that. The date was to be from the last day of the GG's ColoRODo show and arriving in Bowling Green, just in time for their "Nostalgia Drags and show" event the next weekend. The whole trip was going to take five days and would stop at various shops, manufacturers and car collections along the way.

Dan and I thought that'd be a real kick, traveling with a whole bunch of rodders, seeing the sites along the way and checking out some collections. By signing up (and paying tour costs up front), lodging and most meals were taken care of - simply pack your bags, fuel up the car and enjoy the five day, 1500 mile trip with others. We sent in our registration money for the 'Hall of Fame Road Tour' (there was a limit of 50 cars on this tour) and looked forward to the September GG's show in Loveland and then the start of the tour. We'd decided to take my '55 Cadillac and ride together. Shouldn't be a problem since the Cadillac was a proven highway traveler, besides, GG's had planned for a "rescue" trailer to follow the group in case anyone had any problems. The first stop on the tour was The Vehicle Vault car collection in Parker, Colorado, only about 20 miles from my home. Being it was so close, we decided not to go to The Ranch on Sunday and we'd meet the group in Parker. Our first stop for the evening would be the Holiday Inn atop Raton Pass, just south of Trinidad, CO. It would take us about four hours of driving to get there from Parker. What I didn't know at the time was that this trip was to be on Interstates-all the way and I hate Interstates but thought this would be the one time that it would be OK especially seeing 50 hot rods and classic vehicles all together heading down the highway. Boy was I wrong!

Dan and I took the "back way" from Parker to ColoRODo Springs since the traffic between Denver and the Springs on I-25 is nuts. If you like driving at 90 mph for 60 miles, then I-25 should be your playground. I don't like it so I go a different way. Once past the Springs, the Interstate highway is reasonably flat until you get near Trinidad. At this point, the Sangre DeCristo mountains loomed in front of us and Raton Pass is at an elevation of 7835 feet. Up and over is the only way and the New Mexico state border is at the top of the pass. Funniest thing is Dan and I only saw a couple of the tour cars pass us on the tour as we drove. What happened to everyone? By the time we got to the motel, 80% of the "tour group" was already there. Guess by taking the back way, we must've been the last in line. Oh well, in the morning we were scheduled to take a two-lane and it'd be fun running with the whole group.

The motel atop Raton Pass had our rooms ready (reservations were made by GG's staff as well as most food along the way - part of the registration fee) and at 7PM dinner was being served in one of the convention rooms. After that, some of the participants headed for the bar but since Dan and I are not drinkers, we headed for our room. A 7:30AM 'driver's meeting' the next morning would come early.

Day 2, Trinidad to Amarillo. 380 miles. After the driver's meeting and the day's stops explained, the tour group got into our cars and headed south. Our first scheduled stop would be Santa Rosa, NM and "Bozo's" car collection-The Route 66 museum. Just south of Las Vegas, NM, we grabbed highway 84, a 41 mile two-lane short cut that headed southeast for I-40. Most of the cars on the tour stayed together until we got to Santa Rosa and arrived about 10am. Bozo had coffee and donuts and cookies for us while we viewed his collection. Dan and I had met Bozo (yes, that's his name!) when my '55 Cadillac had been invited to the indoor show in Albuquerque earlier in the year.

Shortly after we arrived, several of the tour group left, we were to find out later that those guys - a few Camaros, couple of Corvettes, couple of hot rods and a few trucks, would always run way past the speed limit on the Interstate and it seemed like they were always the first to get to the next stop. The funniest thing I saw on this leg of the trip was that the 'rescue vehicle', sponsored by the Greening Rod Shop in Nashville, TN, was among the guys that left first! I wondered how the rescue vehicle would rescue someone that had trouble behind them. The 'tour' continued east to Glen Rio, NM, and the Russell truck stop for lunch. Dan and I were the last ones to leave Bozo's as I had to get some fuel. My Cadillac's limit is about 200 miles so we decided to forego Glen Rio and continue on into Amarillo. Our next stop was the Cadillac Ranch outside of Amarillo. Dan and I walked out to where the Cadillacs were buried nose first. I can't understand why so many people wantonly destroy a landmark, just to place their names, which will be sprayed over by the next visitor. There was so much spray paint on what's left of those Cadillacs it was over an inch thick in some places, probably the only thing holding them together.

Our over-night stop, the Holiday Inn, wasn't far away from the next collection - Bill's Backyard Classics in south Amarillo. What a collection it was -- '50's and '60's Cadillacs, Oldsmobiles and more '61 Pontiacs than I've ever seen in one spot. Dinner was at Mark Warrick's private collection on the western edge of Amarillo. Mark's got some great projects ranging from '57 Chevys to chopped Mercs but he really likes '62 Chevys - 409's and the like.

Day 3, Amarillo to Oklahoma City. 300 miles. We were looking forward to visiting Owen's Salvage Yard in Wellington, Texas, 130 miles east and south of Amarillo. Flat Top Bob, a friend I'd met years ago at the HAMB drags, greeted us as we pulled in. He allowed any and all of us to check out his yard or simply wander around it. Most of the tour were invited to take one of several junkyard vehicles and drive up and down the rows of 40s, 50s and 60s derelict cars. Later that morning Bob hosted lunch at his private "estate" just a few blocks from the yard. After checking out his personal collection of cars, old signs and a delicious lunch, goodbyes were said and most of the tour were off to Clinton, OK, to the Route 66 Museum and Car Collection. For the second day in a row, I'd had enough Interstate driving so asked Dan to find me a two lane highway while I put fuel in my Cadillac. The thing that disappointed me after two days on the road was that few of the other drivers traveled together. It seemed no one wanted to stay in a group. Dan and I drove by ourselves 85% of the time. Okay, time to make our own 'fun.'

From Wellington east, Dan and I drove the Cadillac the rest of our 185 mile trip on two-lane highways and would you believe Oklahoma has mountains? Yep, we could see 'mountains' in the distance and our two-lane took us through them. The Wichita Mountains rise to 2423 feet on the flat plains, sticking up like a sore thumb - wouldn't see that on the Interstate. Something else not seen over the Interstate: a B-52 and two C-130 transports doing low level passes over some acreage. We approached Oklahoma City from the south and found our final destination for the night, the Hilton Garden Inn at 4:30 PM. At 5:30, we drove to the Ted Davis collection. Ted's into 1930's Packards, has some wonderful Brass Era cars and a great shop. Dinner was served at 6 and since Dan and I were last in line after touring his facility (Dan has to read almost everything posted on the walls!), most of the tables were full so we were allowed to eat in Ted's massive paneled office on his beautiful wooden conference table! Felt like VIP's…such a deal!

Day 4, Oklahoma City to Memphis. 550 Miles. This was by far the longest one day drive. Once again it was Interstate and Dan and I simply don't drive 90 mph, so I knew we'd never make the 5:30 dinner at George Poteet's place in Mississippi (we're old, so we poke along at about 70-75 mph!).

Thirty-seven miles past the Arkansas line, I got tired of the crowded Interstate and eighteen wheelers. I needed fuel again, besides, the rest of the group was miles ahead. Once again Dan and I were driving by ourselves. Dan, my excellent map-reading navigator found me a two-lane, great for a bit of sightseeing which the Interstate didn't have. A couple of miles south of Ozark, Arkansas - Highway 64 – we drove a nice curvy, hilly highway ran through several small towns. Approaching Conway, at about 1 pm, I heard a growling noise. Pulling into a WalMart parking lot to check it out I found the A/C compressor bearing smoking. Ooops, better fix that - an O'Reilly's auto parts store was just a few blocks away. The A/C compressor and the power steering are run off one belt on my 500" Cadillac engine and the alternator on another. I had to eliminate the A/C and find a shorter belt to run power steering only. Dan and I got out the tool box and scoped out the situation –shouldn't be too tuff to change the belt. Wrong! The engine in my Cadillac had apparently settled on the mounts since I put the car on the street in 2010. The crank pulley was only a quarter of an inch above the saddle. The belt is at least 5/8 inch thick-no way to remove it. Guess we'll get at it from the bottom. Jack the car up, put a jackstand under it and put a blanket on the ground. The first thing I had to do was remove the lower part of the radiator shroud, once that was out of the way, I loosened the power steering pump and removed the fan as the belt wouldn't go over the fan, then I removed the bolts from the crank pulley. With all that out of the way, Dan took the belt into the O'Reilly's to find a shorter belt. He came back with three. We had to try each one and adjust the power steering pump each time to see if that particular belt would work. Of course, the third one was the correct one- it tightened up fine. Took an hour to put it all back together. When I was done I was able to wash my hands in the store's bathroom, paid for the belt and thanked the gentlemen in the store for the use of their lot and bathroom. Three hours later we were back on the road. I've always said "If you can't fix your hot rod on the side of the road, you'd best stay home." I don't like staying home! The best part of this breakdown was Dan asking just after we'd pulled into the O'Reilly's parking lot was 'Do you think the support trailer would come rescue us?" To which I replied "The GG's support truck/trailer is 100 or so miles ahead of us! Doubt they'd come back."

The worst part of this stretch of driving wasn't the A/C problem, it was the Interstate. Near Memphis we had to get back on the Interstate to get through Memphis as our over-night stop was east of Memphis. Around 8PM, in the dark, forty miles west of Memphis we sat in a traffic jam for the better part of half an hour - eighteen wheelers in front of us, in back and alongside. We were boxed in and going nowhere fast. It wasn't so much the jam that was bad, it was the highway --the Interstate had had the patches patched and those patches were patched again. There wasn't a smooth spot in either lane. It's a good thing we crawled through it, would've shaken all the dead bugs out of my Caddy's grille. My brother and I finally rolled into the Hampton Inn in Collierville, east of Memphis at 9:30PM, hungry and tired.

Day 5, Collierville to Bowling Green. 300 miles. At the final driver's meeting, our Tour Guide Ed Capen thanked everyone for going and discussed the possibility of next year's tour. The group loaded up and drove back into Memphis to tour Comp Cams. Not us! Dan and I decided to forego driving back into Memphis and went south out of Collierville on a two-lane instead. I simply wasn't going to get on another Interstate. If I was going to drive by myself again, I figured we'd take the scenic way. We took Highway 57 east, a few miles north of the Mississippi border. The 90 miles was very scenic, small towns are a joy to drive through, especially in a 1955 Cadillac – people stop in their tracks, jaws drop, thumbs-up are shown. At the gas stations, we are a car show! Highway 128 north took us across the PickWick Dam and Lake into Savannah, TN. Just past Waynesboro we grabbed the Natchez Trace Parkway -70 miles of nothing but curves, hills, trees and zero traffic ending just 15 miles south of Nashville! Just as Dan and I were getting back on I-65 in Nashville, several of the tour group passed us and we followed them into Greening Auto Company in Nashville, our lunch stop. After touring Greening's rod building shop (their claim to fame is they built a Ridler winner a few years ago), Dan and I took 31W north (a two-lane) out of Nashville headed for Bowling Green. Sixty miles later, just as we were getting onto I-65, again, several members of the tour passed us and we followed them to the Holley Performance Manufacturing facility. After the tour, we weren't very far from the Holiday Inn University Plaza Motel, our final destination. The tour group stayed there for the weekend, each making the morning trek to Beech Bend Raceway, the Nostalgia Nats and Good-Guy's weekend event.

Monday morning. Bowling Green, Kentucky. By the time Dan and I rolled out of bed, had breakfast and proceeded to haul our bags to the car, only two of the tour group remained in the parking lot. Everyone else had already left. We headed to the nearby Corvette Museum, the Corvette factory and drove up to Mammoth Caves –last time we were there was in 1995. Later that afternoon, we drove south for Tennessee to see Alan Mayes, Editor of CK Deluxe and Ol' Skool Rodz magazines. In the late afternoon we found a motel in Tullahoma, called Alan and agreed to meet for breakfast then take a quick tour of his home and cars. Later that afternoon, we drove south to Lynchburg and did a Jack Daniels Distillery tour. On the way back north we toured the George Patton museum within the Ft. Knox/U.S. gold bullion depository. After sightseeing around the area all week, we ended up in Fairmont, Indiana, for the James Dean Festival and drove over to Gas City for the Ducktail event-both shows within five miles of each other. On Monday, we headed home for Denver, ColoRODo, a long two-day drive. When I pulled into my garage, the trip odometer read 13 miles short of 4,000.

THE TETON INCIDENT

Brakes are a needed thing on any hot rod or kustom, but working brake lights prevent rear-end collisions wherever you go. We'd been wanting to go back to Puyallup, Washington for the Good-guys event there so we decided to take only one car this time –Dan's '64 Chevy Impala Super Sport. He'd had some major work done on the car so we wouldn't have any problems on the road. However, Murphy is always present on ANY trip.

July, 2017. Jenny Lake, Wyoming. On the second day of our "vacation," Dan's brake lights failed to work. We'd stopped at the Entrance to the Grand Teton National Park to shoot some pix in front of the sign. Dan stayed in the car and I got out with the camera to record the fact that we'd driven his 1964 Impala SS from Denver, ColoRODo. Actually, the Teton's weren't as far as we were going – we planned to be in Seattle, Washington for the Good-guys event in the suburb of Puyallup on Thursday, in time for the kick-off party.

Prior to us getting on the road, on the Saturday before we were to leave on Monday, July 24, we installed a Dakota Digital cruise control. *Personal promotional note: These units are the best ones on the market today.* Anyway, there are two wires that are required to be connected to the brake switch. The brake switch on a '64 is easy to get at and simple in operation- a plunger that fits against the brake pedal and a nut to hold it on the bracket. Depress the brake pedal, the plunger drops out and makes electrical contact, illuminating the brake lights. The wires are to cut off the cruise control when the brake pedal is pushed. It's a two wire connection. Easy as pie. After the rest of the installation, that was simple. I hooked the two wires up to the brake wires and told Dan we were done, we'd take the car for a test drive. Out to the highway, the cruise worked fine-hit the button and it immediately kicked in. Held the speed with no problems. Two miles down the road I told Dan to tap the brake, see if it would disconnect. Yep, worked like a charm…now we're ready to go!

On Monday, heading north on Highway 230 in Wyoming, Dan had to tap the brake to slow for a car in front of him but it wouldn't disconnect. He had to really push down on the brake to disconnect it, almost like slamming on the brakes. "What the hell?" I asked. "You should only have to tap it slightly to disconnect it…just like when we test drove it."

"Well, it's not working like that," Dan replied.

"OK, when we get fuel, let me check the wiring on the brake switch. Maybe it vibrated loose or I didn't have the wire all the way into the butt connector."

At the gas station, I got out of the car first before Dan had to move the car to a different pump cuz the one he was at wasn't working. He pulled the car forward and stopped. Ooooops, no brake lights! Maybe that's why the cruise control isn't working correctly. After he got fuel, I crawled under the dash and checked the wires. They were connected and tight. "Dan,' I said, pushing the switch plunger in and out, "Check the brake lights now."

"They're working," he said.

"Hmmmmmm, they weren't a minute ago. They didn't illuminate when you moved the car."

"Well, they are now!"

Back on the road we talked about the switch and how they are prone to burn out. We thought maybe we'd better find a NAPA store and purchase another and change it out. Well, ya know how that goes, right? We forgot. Tuesday morn we left Riverton, Wyoming after our over-night there, headed down the road, not even thinking about the cruise control since it had been working well. That is, until we stopped in front to the Teton sign and I noticed the brake lights not working at all…and you do not want ANY tourists following you through the Tetons simply cuz they are not watching your rear-end-they're looking at the mountains…!!! Dan remembered he had another one in the trunk, but wasn't certain it was a new one or a used one.

"Get it out of the trunk and I'll change it right here before we go further," I said. Dan unloaded the trunk, found the switch. After I examined it, it looked like a new one, still in the box it came from

NAPA in and felt like it was working OK.. Under the dash, I unhooked the wires, twisted the nut off of it and pulled it out. Hooked up the new one, pushed the plunger in and out - it felt good. "Brake lights working?" I yelled from under the dash.

"Yep, working fine."

I bolted it back in, hooked the wires up and we put everything back into his trunk. Problem solved.

Since we were near the Teton Mountains, we didn't need the cruise control. Cruise control is best on flat highways, especially when there's nothing to see. Around the Tetons were tons of tourists-have to watch out for most of them so no need for the cruise! The only important thing was the brake lights worked!

After a five mile traffic jam getting into downtown Jackson on the two-lane (it started raining late afternoon as we were driving next to the Tetons so all the tourists decided to head back to their motel rooms) we found a NAPA store and bought a new brake switch, just in case.

Didn't think much about it after that. We drove to Driggs, Idaho, on the way to Rexburg. There were a couple of scenic areas we stopped at and I noticed the brake lights worked sometimes and sometimes not...guess that switch was bad as well, good thing we bought a new one. We eventually drove out of the rain and stayed over-night in Rexburg, figured I'd better change that switch again. Dan got the new one out and I checked it-it didn't feel good for some reason, but I figured it should be good since it was new. Not so fast! Just because it's new doesn't mean it's any good! Don't have much of a choice-the other one is bad so I put in the new switch, tossed the other two in the trash.

Wednesday morn, we headed out across the Idaho plains, drove north into Montana and just as quickly back into Idaho to go over Lolo Pass. From Lolo Pass, it's all downhill for 99 miles – no need for cruise control. That drive took us all day and there were lots to see on the way, we over-nighted in Lewiston, Idaho. Thursday morn we drove into Washington State, took a bunch of two-lanes and ended up in Ellensburg for gas. From there it's only about 90 miles, we'd be in Puyallup early afternoon.

The fair-grounds in Puyallup is huge with lots of cruising lanes - you could cruise around all day if you wanted to. There's an "indoor" car show as well as all the parking areas throughout the grounds and a huge vendor area inside too. I'd say the whole fair-grounds is at least as big as the Des Moines, Iowa, fair-grounds. Good-guys registered close to 3000 cars for the event.

Friday and Saturday went fast-as we were heading out Saturday night for something to eat, Dan remembered we needed another brake lite switch so we went looking for a NAPA store-didn't find one but we found an Auto Zone. They had a switch by a different manufacturer. Dan bought it, we got something to eat and went back to the fair-grounds cuz they have a nighttime "cruise" through and around a kiddie ride area called "Sillyville" and a live band. This goes on until 11:00 PM and hundreds of cars participate.

Sunday morn we drove to the fair-grounds to view the award winners. We'd hoped to win the Long Distance award but Dan got beat out of the "Long Distance" award by 50 miles. After viewing all the award cars, we were sitting on a bench in the fair-grounds looking at the map trying to figure the best way to get to downtown Seattle cuz we had a 'all day whale watching cruise' scheduled for 7:45 AM the next morning and motel reservations only 12 blocks from Pier 69. Dan happened to look over at the '64 from the bench. "Look, the brake lights are on."

"Now we know that brake switch is not any good," I said.

"Look, they went out by themselves," Dan remarked.

"Not good. Where's that new switch? I'd better change it, don't want this one short-circuiting and burning out the wiring. Besides, if we're going to downtown Seattle, we NEED brake lights," I said.

Laying on my back, again, for the third time this trip, I swapped the switch. This one felt better than the last one from NAPA-at least, the plunger moved freely. We checked the taillights operated by the switch several times and it seemed to work well. Mind at ease, we headed for downtown Seattle.

That was half of our two week trip. On Monday we did an all-day boat tour to some of the islands north of Seattle and we did the Boeing airplane factory tour in Everett on Tuesday. From there we headed east, taking our time seeing the sights and arrived back in Riverton, Wyoming, on Friday for another car show. Dan won "Best GM" at that show but got beat out for the Long Distance award again by a car from Evergreen, ColoRODo. On Sunday, we made the 8 hour trip home. Never had another problem with the brake switch or the cruise control.

A bit of a preface to the following story. Dan wanted to write a story he dreamed up in 2010. So I (Roger) told him to sit down and write it and I'd help him with the punctuation, etc. It took him a few days to write this one and I was surprised it was such a long story - I kinda figured it'd just be a short story but Dan figured out the action and the plot for this story by himself. Read on...

THE LONGEST DAY

A hot rod story by DAN JETTER.

Eddie was a wildcat. He didn't like authority, or the people that forced it upon him. He'd been in and out of foster homes from the age of eleven, after his parents were killed in an automobile crash and there were more than a few trips to juvie, before his eighteenth birthday. He and his younger brother, by two years, were separated after that fateful day. He didn't know where Vinnie had been sent, but he vowed one day he would track him down.

When Eddie turned eighteen he was out on his own, finally, out of the last miserable family that called itself Foster Care. All those Foster Care "Parents" over the years reminded him too much of his Father, Theodore Magnotti. He was a powerful attorney and Mother-Janet, was a High School teacher, both strict disciplinarians and nothing out of the normal was tolerated.

He'd been hanging with some of his buddies since he was old enough to get his driver's license. Everyone that was anyone, hung out at T.O.'s restoration shop and Eddie finally talked T.O. into giving him a job after his final year in school. He got all the odd jobs. T.O. was short for Tony Orofina, the owner. He owned a bad-ass chopped '49 Mercury. It wasn't the engine that made it bad-assed cuz it had the usual flathead with all the goodies stuffed inside and it was slammed on the ground with wide whites and caps. What made it bad was the Ocean Mist Green paint with the wildest lime green flame job this side of the Mississippi. T.O. and the guys would cruise in that Mere every night of the week and all weekend. They were always looking for something new to get into-a race, another new project or anything that could keep them on the edge and ahead of everyone else.

Little Davy worked at the shop with T.O. and got along good with Eddie. Eddie was really interested in the old cars these guys were fixing up and putting back on the road. Out back of the shop was a good assortment of early iron T.O.'d collected over the years. A chopped, unfinished '34 Ford four door, a couple of Chevy coupes of the forties, Model A's - both coupes and sedans, a couple of bullet-nose Studebakers, a '51 Merc four door and a parts car to go with it and six mid-fifties Cadillacs in various state of disrepair. Farther in the back of the lot were three shoebox Fords, and eight '55-'57 Chevys including a convert and a Nomad wagon. There was enough vintage tin to keep T.O.'s guys busy for years. Best part-if they didn't have it they could probably find it.

Little Davy was the proud owner of a chopped, channeled '36 Dodge pickup sporting a 392" Hemi. It ran big and little wide whites and '56 Olds Fiesta caps. The seat was a colorful Mexican blanket and the floor was made from yield signs, the door panels were speed limit signs. The bed had been narrowed and the rear tires were tucked tight against the bed. It was just big enough to haul a cooler and lawn chairs, maybe a small tool box in the corner. Little Davy didn't drive it much because he'd gained some weight and couldn't quite fit under the steering wheel and/or bend enough to get in the cab. He was looking to build himself a bigger and roomier ride, maybe do one of the Caddys. He figured on no chopped top, but maybe slammed on the ground and move the seat back three, four inches to give him more stomach and leg room. He and Eddie walked T.O.'s back yard, looking.

Eddie really liked the looks of the rat rods that a few guys were building lately and he had his eye on one of the A's out back. He figured a sedan would be the ticket for him. Lots of leg room, he could chop it a few inches and still not be cramped up inside it. Of course it had to have a severe channel job on it, too. He and T.O. worked out a deal on one of the better of the sedans. As the months rolled by, Eddie worked on it after hours. T.O. and Little Davy would stop by after dinner and cruising to see how he was progressing on it. He'd chopped it three inches, channeled the body six inches, and stuck a Ford 9 inch Posi with Moser axles and 4:11 gears out back. The front was a Super Bell dropped axle with disc brakes for quicker stopping. The suspension was set up with a four-bar and airbags in the rear. He found a big block Chevy 409" with dual Carter AFB's, 425 HP, and stuck it between the rails. Behind that power was a Muncie

M-22 "Rock Crusher" 4-speed with an 11 inch clutch and pressure plate covered by an Ansen scattershield. He ran wide whites on steel wheels, spider caps and trim rings. The rear tires were pie crust Firestone cheater slicks, ready for any street race that might arise at a moment's notice.

Eddie took a break from building it one Friday night and he, T.O., and Little Davy, cruised out to the local hangout-- 4B's-- "Billy Bob's Burger Barn", to see what was going on. Four B's was the place to be seen and stop to say hi to your buddies hanging out for the evening. It was the place to get to know some of the local cruisers. The usual assortment of 'Stangs, Camaros, Tri-Five Chevys, Mopars, a few Corvettes, some A's, a different assortment of trucks and other type of vehicles would park and hang out inside and outside on warm nights.

As the warmer months brought longer evenings, 4B's would be packed with cruisers and a lot of locals stopped in to check out all the cool rides in the lot. Eddie and the guys were standing around their cars one long, warm Friday night just BS'ing about work, politics and cars, when they heard a high pitched whine coming off the main street. It rumped, thumped, and growled as it turned down the aisle they were parked in. They watched it kick up parking lot dust from the zoomie exhaust that stuck out from under the fat fenders. The chromed straight axle below the jacked up body they couldn't miss and the bug eyed headlights sitting on top of putrid yellow fenders didn't add any grace to the yellow coupe - it was ugly. They watched it cruise past, the fat rear tires squashing coke cups, fry boxes and malt lids, just idling, shaking the ground they were standing on. It moved on down the aisle and up another aisle looking for a place to park. Little Davy said, to no one in particular, "That's one bitchin' Willys gasser."

Eddie piped up, "That's got to be about a '37 or '8 running some sort of big block and blower. Sure sounds healthy."

"That's a Studebaker my friends, probably a '37 or a '38," T.O. commented. "You don't see many of those early coupes around. Must be a new car or someone just moved here from Cali. It looks like we have new competition boys."

"How do you know it's a Studey?" Little Davy questioned.

"Just from pictures in a Studebaker book. It's probably a Commander model. Let's go scope it out and talk to the dude driving it," T.O. shot back.

They walked down the row of cars and found the coupe parked between a couple of muscle cars. There was already a large crowd around it and the driver. It was like Ghirardelli chocolate in a display case, everyone wanted a piece of it. They worked their way through the crowd and got close enough to check out the front end. Disc brakes on the ends of the shiny, chromed straight axle and steel wheels wrapped in 195x65x15 Goodrich rubber. The interior held a stock looking dash with a huge tach mounted on top, in line with the driver's sight through the windshield. A pod of three gauges to the right of the tach, housing water temp, volts, and oil pressure were also on the top of the dash. There was nice dark brown loop carpet on the floor snuggling up to the 4-speed shifter and the headliner and door panels were done in a light two-tone tan cloth and naugahyde. The bench seat was finished in the same material with a sculptured pattern. Nice enough for a street rod, but overkill in a rat rod. Eddie, Little Davy or T.O. wouldn't be caught dead with that material in one of their cars! But, it looked very functional and comfortable. The steering column was a tilt unit in a chrome finish-more street rod. There was no back seat, just an open area with wheel tubes and a divider between that area and the trunk. The door handles were gone but most bright trim was polished to perfection and still on the car. Out back the rear bumper was nicely chromed with wheelie bars coming out from the underside. In front of that, a narrowed Chevy 12 bolt with humongous slicks with 10x15 chrome wheels filled the widened rear fenders. By the time the guys got around to the passenger's side, the owner had opened the hood. A big block Chevy 427" with a BDS blower sat low into the engine compartment; it looked like it had some set-back to it. Since there was no scoop on the hood, cold air was forced through inlet tubes from the grill to the air cleaner atop the large double pumper carb. Everything on the engine was chromed along with the serpentine belt system and all the pulleys and brackets. The zoomie headers were jet hot coated and didn't look as if there were a lot of miles on them. Matter of fact, it looked more like a gold-chainer's street rod and the car looked as if it was recently finished. This may have been its first time out. After checking out the engine, Eddie glanced around looking for the owner but he'd disappeared into the crowd. Probably went to eat or look at some of the cars he passed when he first turned into the parking lot.

The three of them walked back to their own cars muttering to themselves about the hot new street rod in town. It was late and the cruisers started to leave for other parts of the city known only to them. They hung around for a while, waiting for the owner of the Studebaker coupe to come back but he never did. He was probably standing in the background, simply watching! T.O. and the guys headed for their cars to find some fun somewhere else on the street.

As Eddie pulled onto the street he thought to himself that he should get to know the owner of that Stude gasser. He may be new to the area and not know anyone yet. He'd introduce himself if he comes out to 4B 's again.

A couple of weeks later, back at the shop, Eddie and T.O. were busy working on a couple of customer's cars and chatting about not seeing that Stude coupe back out on the street.

"Hey T.0.," Eddie said. "You think that yellow coupe we saw was built for the strip and not the street? It hasn't been out since that Friday night."

"Can't say," T.O. offered. "Maybe he doesn't know anybody and then maybe he's still working the bugs out of it. Sure didn't look to me like it was a strip beater, more of a street racer. Next time it's out, we'll have to introduce ourselves."

That Friday night they cruised out to 4B's again. It was packed as they pulled in, cruising up and down the rows to find that primo parking place. Finally finding two spaces next to each other, they backed their rods in and parked for the evening. No sooner had Eddie gotten out of his sedan than a kid ran towards him. "Hey you," he yelled, "You can't park there. These are saved."

Eddie turned to see who was yelling. "Who are you, parking lot police?" Eddie sneered, not liking what he was hearing. "I ain't moving from here. I don't see any body's name on this space and if there was, I still wouldn't move. Get lost kid."

"My friend is going to be pissed when he gets here," responded the kid. "I'll tell him what happened and you and him can argue it out."

"Yeah, send him over and we'll discuss it," Eddie shot back. "Man, I hate people that think they control everything."

"Hey, T.O., let's go get a burger and a Coke. That jerk brought my blood to a boiling point, I need something cool."

After finding a spot near the window, small talk ensued until T.O. spotted the Stude. "Hey, check it. Isn't that the yellow Stude?" T.O. asked, looking out the window to see the yellow coupe pull in and stop in front of their cars. The kid that Eddie got into it with, leaned inside the coupe, apparently talking to the driver. He backed away from the car and pointed to the inside seating area, motioning to his hair like he's explaining Eddie's hair to the guy! After a few minutes the driver of the coupe moved down the row of cars and parked on the end. He got out, looking towards the restaurant.

"Looks like he may be coming to find you Eddie," T.O. said.

"Yeah, well, we'll see what he has to say when he finds me," Eddie shot back.

They finished their burgers and Cokes and headed for the door. As they were working their way through the crowd, a young dude with slick-backed black hair, wearing a white t-shirt with rolled up sleeves, sidled up to Eddie. "You the one owning the chopped A sedan down there?"

"Yeah, that's mine. Who's asking?"

"I had my friend save those spots for me and a pal and you ain't him," the dude said.

Well, you got that right, I ain't your friend and it doesn't look like your pal came with you, so, let me tell you how it works around here since you seem to be new to 4B's. Me and my buddy got here first and it's first come gets the parking spot," Eddie snarled. "So what makes you special that you got to have that particular spot for parking your puke yellow coupe there?"

"Whose car you calling Puke Yellow? That's Sunburst Yellow to you," the dude growled. "It's better than that rusty tin box you call a rod. I wouldn't have something that ratty sitting in my garage. l would never own one of those rat rod thingies."

"Puke Yellow, Sunburst Yellow, Chicken Fat Yellow. What's the difference?" Eddie snapped. "That nose bleed high coupe of yours looks like it can only go a block or two and be finished for the day."

"You challenging me to a race, dick head?" The dude asked.

"Dick head? You just call me a dick head, punk. I oughta knock the shit out of you right here," Eddie yelled, giving the dude a push.

T.O. stepped in between them so it didn't go any farther than a couple of shoves. A small crowd formed around them. Eddie and the dude stared at each other wondering who was going to throw the first punch.

"Eddie, be cool," T.O. said. "We don't need to make a scene here. We'll get tossed off the lot and never be able to come back. I know he pissed you off but there's another time and place for this."

"We'll meet again, punk," Eddie yelled to the dude as he backed away. "And, if it's a race you want, I'll give you one, asshole." The dude walked back to his coupe, fired it up, pulled out of the space and nailed it. Smoke and dust filled the air and two black patches of rubber followed the coupe out of the aisle, to the delight of the spectators.

"C'mon Eddie, I'll buy ya a soda and we'll talk about it," T.O. said.

They walked back into the restaurant, found a table by the window and ordered two Cokes.

"Here," T.O. said, shoving a Coke across the table. "Cool off a bit, or I'll dump it down your shirt."

A smile crossed Eddie's face. "Aw, I ain't that hot."

"Do you really want to race that dude in the coupe?" T.O. asked. "I think maybe your sedan can take him, but with that blown 427" it could be a toss-up against your 409". You need to think this one out very carefully before you step into that."

"He really pushed my buttons," Eddie said.

"Yeah, I know," T.O. said. "If that race comes, you've got to have your W-block tuned the best it can be. Make sure those slicks have the right air pressure in them. You'll need to get a good shot off the line. That's very important." Eddie nodded in agreement and smiled again.

T.O. finished his Coke and got up. "Let's go," and headed for the door. The lot was nearly empty. They walked to their rods, got in, fired them up and left. It had been a long evening.

As the days got hotter and Spring morphed into Summer, Eddie kind of forgot about the incident with the coupe dude. T.O. walked up to him as he was doing some body work on a car, "You gonna stay late tonight and tune that big block?"

Not looking up from sanding, Eddie answered, "Yeah, I was thinking about that. I oughta get those tires checked, too! Ya never know if that Yellow coupe will show again this Friday. I definitely want to head out there Friday night since it will be one of the longer days of the year, seems like daylight lasts forever."

"I'll stay late tonight and help," T.O. replied as he headed back to the other side of the shop.

After the shop closed, T.O., Little Davy and Eddie got busy putting a tune-up on that large 409" engine. They installed new plugs and wires, got the distributor dwell tuned correctly, set the timing and did a few adjustments to the big twin Carter carbs. It sounded really good and fired off each time with hardly any cranking. The air was checked in all four tires and the fluids were checked in the tranny and the rear-end, along with the radiator. They were ready for Friday night.

T.O. closed the shop early Friday afternoon. They wanted to get out to 4B's earlier than usual. They knew it was going to be a crowded place because there was going to be a DJ spinning the discs, giving out prizes to participants and they wanted a close-in parking spot.

Eddie cruised his A sedan, and T.O. drove his chopped Mercury. Even Little Davy motored out with his '36 Dodge Brothers pickup, the first time this year. They arrived early enough and found some spots next to the curb, across from the entrance to the restaurant.

Just standing around talking, they heard a whine coming down the street, getting louder as it got closer. They all watched it turn into the lot. It was the Studebaker coupe. It went past them, turned, and then backed in behind them, rear bumper to rear bumper.

Eddie saw the dude get out of the coupe, glance at the guys and start to walk toward them. Eddie was clinching his fist, ready to strike if that dude said something off color. The coupe dude stopped directly in front of them. "Hey, I want to introduce myself and I want to apologize for my rudeness. I think we got off on the wrong foot. My name is Vincent Johansen. I own the '38 Studebaker Commander coupe. What's your name?" he asked, looking directly at Eddie.

Eddie stood there not saying anything when T.O. said, "I'm T.O., short for Tony Orofina. This is Little Davy Jones, and this is Ed... "

"It's Eddie." Eddie interrupted looking into the olive color eyes of Vincent. "Just Eddie."

"Well, just Eddie, it's my pleasure to meet you, especially under a normal circumstance," Vincent said, extending his hand.

Eddie looked at his gesture and made no effort to do the same.

"You challenged me to a race the last time we talked. Do I remember correctly?" Vincent asked, glaring at Eddie.

Eddie nodded.

"You still up for it? Tomorrow night at sunset, out on the old Powerhouse Road. You know where that is?" Vincent asked.

"Yeah, I know where it is," Eddie snarled. "I'll be there, but I'm wonderin', are you as yellow as that coupe of yours?" Eddie raised his voice.

"You'll find out on Saturday night. Just make sure you're on time. I'll be waiting for you and that rusty tin P.O.S. of yours. Oh, and bring your friends too. I want them to see you cringe when I run your ugly sedan into the ground where it belongs," Vincent said. He backed away and turned to head back to his Studebaker.

"You ain't running nobody into the ground," Eddie yelled back.

Eddie looked at T.O., then turned to Little Davy and said. "You gonna be with us tomorrow night, friend, to see some real racing?"

"Hell yes, I'll be there," Little Davy said with a smile on his face. "You know we're friends and friends need to support each other. I wouldn't miss you creaming that ugly Stude for anything!"

That night Eddie couldn't sleep. He tossed and turned all night thinking about the race that was coming. Saturday morning arrived way too soon. It was going to be a long day. He had to finish up a few small things on his car, but in the back of his mind he was worried. Maybe that Stude could take his car... maybe...

The afternoon slipped into the early evening and Eddie was ready to go... he wasn't in any hurry to get to Powerhouse Road, so he kept his speed below the limit. T.O. followed in his chopped Merc with Little Davy riding shotgun.

They were the first to arrive. Powerhouse Road was abandoned. There wasn't a soul in sight, just the way Eddie wanted it. The road was narrow with a drainage ditch on one side. The other side had an old railroad embankment and beyond that, an empty field. About half a mile down the road, a concrete bridge crossed over the meandering drainage ditch. There wasn't enough of a shoulder on either side to pull off onto. The asphalt was rough, but it'd have to do. It'd been filled and patched, some cracks were nothing more than oil and rock, still sticky between the smooth sections. Not so good for Eddie's car, his was lower to the ground than that sky-high coupe.

As they were standing off to the side of the road, they heard the whine of the Studebaker coming from behind them. Vincent stopped in the middle of the intersection and got out. "You ready?" Vincent asked.

"I'm surprised you showed up," Eddie said.

"I see ya brought your buddies. Since I'm alone, T.O. can toss the coin for lane rights and your pal Davy can drop the flag," Vincent said.

"Sounds good to me," T.O. said. "I've got a real silver dollar to use for the coin flip. Been saving it for this special occasion."

"Hate to disappoint you T.O., but this "special occasion" is going to hurt Eddie," Vincent responded. "Uhm, I forgot a flag... Davy, do you have a flag? Wait! T.O., you have any of those red shop rags in that Merc's trunk? Davy can toss or drop that to start the race."

"I think so." T.O. opened the door of the Merc and retrieved a shop rag from under the front seat.

"It's a mile from this intersection to the next one," Vincent explained. "We have the right-away down there. On-coming traffic has to stop. We'll start the race at the bridge, which is a half mile. The first one to the intersection is the winner. Any questions?"

"Why don't we just start from here?" asked Eddie. "Won't your coupe go a mile?"

"Yeah, it will, but the bridge is concrete and makes for a good launch pad," Vincent replied, "Better than this old crummy asphalt."

"Since this is the first day of Summer, it's the longest day of the year. The sun sets at 8:31. That's when we'll start," Vincent continued.

"I'll throw the shop rag in the air," Davy said. "But don't get too squirrely leaving the line, I'll have my back to you so I can watch the cars leave."

"Time for the coin toss. Who's calling it?" T.O. asked.

"Eddie will. He challenged me to this little get-together," Vincent answered quickly. "Call it in the air," T.O. said, as he flipped the coin.

"Tails," Eddie said.

The coin hit the asphalt and bounced once. It rolled toward the Studebaker's tire, ricocheted off it, and dropped. All four of them hurried over to see what came up.

"Tails it is," T.O. said.

"Shit," Vincent muttered.

"I'll take the right lane," Eddie grinned.

The four of them piled into their cars, fired 'em up and idled down to the bridge. The sun was nearing its annual path for the year by the time Eddie and Vincent got lined up.

Little Davy held the red rag high, watching the last sliver of sun disappear beyond the treeless horizon. The seconds seemed like minutes as Eddie's car and Vincent's car warmed up.

Just as the sun disappeared, Davy threw the shop rag in the air. The sound was deafening. Both car's headers belched out a beautiful scream of life. Tire smoke filled the air and the smell of exhaust wafted past Davy and T.O. The race was on!

Eddie's tires grabbed concrete hard and launched like a rocket. Vincent's fat tires fought for some traction, blue smoke boiled off the hides. They finally grabbed and he launched off the concrete trying to catch Eddie. Eddie hit second gear with a half a length ahead of the coupe. The blower on the coupe's engine was gulping for all the air it could get. When Vincent slammed second gear, the coupe started to fly, pulling even with the sedan. Third gear carne quickly in Eddie's sedan and the twin Carters were sucking so hard Eddie thought the manifold would disappear into the engine. They were neck to neck when Vincent hit third gear and started to pull away from Eddie's sedan. Eddie slammed the four-speed into fourth, hoping he could find enough top end to get ahead of Vincent's hard charging coupe. Vincent rapped out that 427" in third gear, watching the tach approach 6,000 RPM's, waiting for the right instant to shift 'cause he knew he didn't have anything after the fourth gear change. The red needle on the tach flew past six, Vincent hit fourth gear and the blower let out a screaming pitch heard for miles. The Stude coupe pulled away from the sedan.

Eddie was worried, maybe the old ugly Stude could beat him ... sure looked like it.

Vincent's coupe had a length on Eddie's lowered sedan when the right rear tire started to disintegrate; shattering the coupe's widened rear fenders. Chunks of rubber flew off the large chrome wheel, smashing into the windshield of Eddie's sedan. It scared the hell of out of him, but he stayed in the throttle hoping he could catch the coupe and pass him before that tire was history. Just as he got alongside the Stude, the tire came flinging off the rim, flying over the top of Eddie's roof

"Oh, shit," Eddie yelled, and ducked. The Studebaker coupe leaned to the right side. Eddie grabbed the shifter and in one quick motion, applied brakes and down-shifted to third gear. The sedan nosed down in front.

The yellow coupe's bare rim dug into the asphalt, spraying sparks to the rear. The front of the Stude came around, crossing into Eddie's lane.

Eddie hit the brakes and down-shifted to second. The transmission growled as it was forced into the lower gear.

Eddie watched in horror as the Stude coupe did a 360 in front of him and then start another one when the naked, bent chrome wheel dug deeper into the asphalt. The coupe flipped twice, slid on the roof and rolled down the embankment. It came to a rest on its roof in the drainage ditch, tires spinning wildly and steam blowing out of the radiator.

Eddie planted both feet on the brake pedal trying to haul the sedan down. It finally slid sideways to a stop. He tossed opened the door and ran for the wrecked coupe.

Back at the start line, T.O. and Davy watched in awe while the coupe flipped and rolled. "C'mon," T.O. yelled. "Better get up there and see if Vincent is hurt." T.O. fired the Merc, as Davy jumped in and hauled ass down to the wreck.

As they came to a screeching, sideways stop, Eddie was already sliding down the embankment into the drainage ditch. The only thing he could see was the Stude's taillights still working.

"Hey, dude, you okay," Eddie asked, trying to see inside the coupe.

"Hell no, I'm not okay," Vincent yelled, trying to get his seat belt unfastened. "Get me the hell out of this thing."

T.O. and little Davy slid down the bank to help Eddie while he worked to release the belt.

"Anybody got a knife and a flashlight?" Eddie asked. "I'm going to cut the belt!"

"Do what you want. Just don't cut me," Vincent yelled.

Davy reached into his pocket and pulled out a six inch blade and handed it to Eddie. He handed the flashlight to Vincent that he took out of T.O.'s glove box.

Eddie groped around until he felt the belt. He started to slice through the belt webbing while T.O. held Vincent up so he wouldn't crash into the water when the belt was cut.

The water in the ditch was about eighteen inches deep, and the roof of the car was submerged in the murky, dark water. Vincent's hair was wet and they didn't want to drop him head first into that crap, so Little Davy forced open the passenger door and helped T.O. hold Vincent.

Eddie finally cut through the belt webbing. T.O. and Davy had a good grip on Vincent as they pulled him out the driver's door and got him on his feet. The four of them worked their way back up the bank.

"Damn, that must have been one hell of a ride, man," T.O. said looking at Vincent. Vincent gazed at T.O., but didn't respond to what was just said. He felt a little woozy, like he was going to pass out.

"Hey, Vincent," Eddie said. "You sure you're okay?"

They sat Vincent down on the asphalt. Eddie looked at T.O. "Think we need an ambulance?"

"He could be going into shock," T.O. said. "Lay him down. See if his head has any bumps on it."

"Where am I?" Vincent asked. "What just happened? My head is spinning in every different direction at once. Who are you guys?"

"Do you know your name?" Eddie asked.

"It's Vinnie. Vinnie Magnotti." Vincent muttered. "Are we home, Eddie?"

Eddie was stunned. Did he hear Vincent say his last name was Magnotti?

"Magnotti?" Eddie asked. "Did he say his last name was Magnotti.

"Yeah he did." T.O. answered. "That's your last name."

"And he said his name was Vinnie." Eddie said in disbelief. "I used to call my kid brother Vinnie all the time."

Little Davy looked at Eddie with a puzzled look on his face, he wasn't following any of the conversation!

"You know what? After all these years, I think I just found my long, lost brother," Eddie said, excited about the prospect.

"Anyone see any cuts on Vinnie's head?" T.O. asked.

Powerhouse Road was black as ink, no lights anywhere to see if Vinnie was cut or bleeding. T.O. walked over to the Merc and switched on the headlights.

Vincent slowly sat up. The three guys surrounded him, examining his clothes for blood.

"What are you looking at?" Vincent asked.

"Is your last name Magnotti or Johansen?" Eddie asked.

"It's Magnotti. That's the name I put on my driver's license," Vincent responded. "My adoptive parents insisted on their name, but I changed my last name when I turned sixteen and got my license. I used my real birth name."

"So you can really be my long lost brother," Eddie said.

"I guess. I had a gut feeling we knew each other from someplace," Vincent said, feeling a bit better. "That first night out at 4B's was a kind of deja vu to me."

"Well, you got my temperament, that's for sure," Eddie replied.

"What are we going to do with the Studebaker, now that it's kind of wrecked and upside down in the ditch?" Davy asked. "We ought to get it out of there right away before the cops find out about this little race!".

"Don't worry about that coupe. I'll call my tow guy and he can come out and get it, take it to the shop." T.O. said. "Now that the two of you really are brothers, you'll have a place to work on it whenever you want. You and Eddie can relive your pasts while you work on your cars."

"Hey, if Vincent is okay and we're finished here, let's head back into town and stop at 4B's for some grub. All this excitement has made me hungry," Little Davy said.

Eddie helped Vincent climb into his sedan, and T.O. and Little Davy slid into the Mercury. They headed for the Drive-in. Half a mile past the bridge they passed the tow truck on its way to retrieve the Stude.

ONE MORE STORY!

The following story is a long way away from a road incident, but it does have a 'road' in the title and I think it is actually kind of funny in a strange way. This story was written in 1997/1998 when I was working for 11 of Primedia's business to business magazines here in Denver (I was Advertising Manager and handled all the advertising placement in all 11 monthly magazines). I used to get on the Monster job site (anyone remember Monster?) chat board and look at other jobs cuz my job was too easy and I had a ton of extra time during the day.

I 'met' Lance Martin on the chat board and come to find out he was taking a course on learning to write fiction...as was I at the time. We hit it off and chatted daily and he eventually suggested we write a story together...if I remember correctly, he'd write a paragraph, send it to me and then I'd write a paragraph and send the whole thing back to him. To say the story got way off track of the original plot would be an understatement. I recall it took us several months to write this story.

When Primedia decided to move its entire operation to Atlanta in early 1999, they offered me a 'better' job in Atlanta and I said, "Not just no, but Hell NO!" With that, I helped them transition everything to Atlanta and I got a nice severance package, stayed in Denver, retired from work(ing ever again) on that last day and started my writing career. I 'polished' this story some months after I left the company and submitted it to several places but no one ever picked it up! SO, for the very first time in nearly 20 years, "Murder on Dirt Road" finally gets published. Hope you enjoy it!

MURDER ON DIRT ROAD

By Roger Jetter and Lance Martin
Copyright 1999/2017 R.A. Jetter and Lance Martin

The coroner zipped the black body bag closed. A detective shot Polaroid's of body parts and evidence notes around the room, to be later scoured for clues. Each flash a shocking memory, capturing a portion of carnage along with the appropriate ID. Ejected photos broke the unnerving silence.

A bloody meat cleaver; the murder weapon, stuck upright in the cutting board and a mottled footprint the only clues. The overfilled sink dripped onto yellow linoleum, creating a crimson stream of blood trickling into the hall. I flipped the disposal switch. Metal teeth chewed potato peel and beef fat as a whirlpool drained the sink. The stench of dishwater filled the kitchen. It was a welcome smell.

My name's Jerry. I'm a part-time detective and fry cook in this lumber mill of a town and I'd been walking Betsy for only fifteen minutes, yet in that time things had changed forever. The Beagle had gotten fidgety as we strolled by Maggie's house. Guess the dog knew something was amiss. I couldn't get her to stop whining or looking back...not even coercing with her favorite hot dog from the souvenir shop helped. Funny how things fall into place, especially when you're a detective with a critical eye...I noticed Maggie's front door open...thought it out of place for a woman that hadn't been outside her home for years. But we kept walking, I'd check later.

Betsy whimpered, tried to tell me something. Dogs have an uncanny sense of knowing things-- unusual behavior, skittish jumps and random barking are often disregarded by humans. "Betsy's seeing Bigfoot again" my wife would say every time the dog jumped on the overstuffed chair and barked at the old growth forest out the patio window. 'Course, twelve foot hairy creatures I do not believe in, but Betsy had been going out of her little dog mind, almost if someone shadowed us that evening as we walked. I'd never seen the dog so agitated. Yet, thinking back on it, I blame myself, we should have stopped when I noticed the door ajar. I'd made it a habit over the years to check in on Maggie. I'd befriended her...and Betsy, of course, loved that old lady. Maggie was eighty, needed someone to look after her, make sure everything was OK. With no relatives, she'd been alone far too many years. No one I knew in this town would hurt Maggie. But we didn't stop and now I wouldn't have to any longer. I felt responsible.

The homicide call came just as we'd gotten home. Told them I'd be right there. I trotted the fifteen blocks back to Maggie's house. After spending too much time in the kitchen surveying the bloody scene, I went to headquarters to sort out this senseless murder. It's not an easy thing when a crime turns ugly. Uglier yet with no clues.

The scariest part was that Maggie wasn't the only one, her death was the third in three weeks. The M.O. matched. Someone was killing helpless old women. The murderer was psycho, elusive and left few clues. In fact, each crime scene had been scoured; each drop of blood, each microfilament lifted and scrutinized by experts in forensic technology. Yet, there was nothing conclusive, except the footprint...one near-perfect, bloody footprint. Surprisingly, in all three homes, almost like the killer purposely placed it. The boot, according to forensics, was a basic steel-toed Wolverine. It appeared the killer took precious minutes to press his size tens into a pool of blood.

That bothered me...why would a boot-print be deliberately placed? Seventy-five percent of the men in this dirty northwest lumber-mill town wore Wolverines, including me, and there were a few women, manly women walking logs in the pond, that wore tens. That alone didn't help. But, there's the other thing that bothered me, no one else noticed, but I did. Maggie had just finished dinner. And so had Cheryl Ann. And the first victim, Beth, was apparently washing dishes when she was murdered...that told me each knew the murderer and trusted them to come into their homes. A place at each table had been set and each had cooked for two people. Three spinsters couldn't eat that much combined. It had to be a male that cut them up. Women aren't that physical.

PING! It hit me. I pushed back from my desk, grabbed car keys, and rushed down the stairs. I couldn't believe I missed it. I almost ran over my partner Arnold as I flew through the station's double doors.

"Whoa Jerry, where you going?" he yelled, trying to regain his balance.

"Hey Arn. Jump in. I'll explain on the way."

Arnie scooted into the passenger seat of the Omomqua County cruiser. He was the epitome of a small town cop. Ex all-star high school quarterback, pro football running back standout that blew out his knee three years into the game ruining any chance of retiring famous and wealthy. At 34, he was big and strong. Muscles built lugging logs at a summer job for his father remained. "What the hell is going on, Jerry?"

"We missed something."

"What? Missed what?"

"No, not missed. Didn't look." I slid the gearshift into low, squealed away from the curb and almost nailed the meter maid. "At all three murders there were two place-settings but only one set of silverware on the table. None in the dishwater...or the trash, remember? One set missing, we never checked to see if any other silverware was missing."

"So, who cares if a few pieces of cheap silverware were missing?"

"No one. Except it wasn't cheap silver, these gals had the real thing."

"Real thing? What you goin' on about, Jer?"

"Silver...antique. Heirloom quality. Maggie was proud of hers. It was a gift from the King of Prussia." If I were correct, silver pieces would be missing from the other victim's homes. I'd venture the male they invited to share their last meal would pawn the antiques sooner or later. When that happened, I'd be ready.

Banging a tire on the log stop at road's edge, I slammed the gearshift into Park, jumped out of the cruiser and bounded over the ditch. If I were the murderer, I'd go out Maggie's screen-less back door with my priceless Prussian plunder, wrapped in the victim's apron. Hopefully, there'd be a missed clue back there...somewhere. I yelled at Arnie; "Go inside, count the place-settings in the China Cabinet."

I scoured the back yard. Walked the fence line like a drill sergeant eyeing his men. Scanned nook and cranny. Every square inch got the once over from my laser-repaired eyes. But, there were no new clues back there. Nothing hiding in the fence holes, no tracks leading out the back gate in the shadow of yesterday's snow. I surmised the silver could be buried for later retrieval. We needed a metal detector.

"They're missing!" Arnie yelled as he rounded the house.

"All of it?"

"One salad fork, one dinner fork, one dessert fork. A teaspoon, coffee spoon, a butter knife, and one dessert knife."

"Hot damn, I was right." The killer had taken one complete place-setting, but why? I guessed 'souvenirs'. "Arnie, you have a metal detector?"

"Yeah, but Bud's got it. I can bring it tomorrow. Have to go to the ranch...an' that's thirty miles of switchbacks from here."

That wasn't going to work, we needed to find the silver today. Tonight. Tomorrow would be too late and there may be another victim by then. "Arnie, we're going to see old Fritz. Is your gun loaded?" The Chief considered Arnie his own personal affliction, his own inept Barney Fife of Mayberry fame. He usually didn't let Arnie have bullets...he'd shot at too many things plunging through the woods surrounding our town way too many times. The citizenship complained someone was going to get shot serious-like. Arnie swore those many times he was only protecting the town from Sasquatch. I just figured he saw ghosts -- old loggers crushed by a falling tree or drowned in the pond. This town was full of those stories. Nevertheless, right now I've got a bigger riddle to solve and thankfully, Arnie's gun wasn't loaded. Fritz Hatchett disliked him intently and I wasn't sure why the Chief hired him.

"Fritz will have a metal detector in that shop of his," I said. Arnie snorted. We crunched through the snow-covered yard toward the car.

Fritz was a gruff old guy of 89. The local repairman that fixes anything -- toasters to TV sets, in the back of his alley shack home.

He'd have whatever working right as rain before you could say Waxahachie Wallbanger. There was another reason to see him. He was the local Bigfoot expert. No one knew Sasquatch like Fritz Hatchett...and I was starting to have strange ideas...always trusted my hunches.

I got lost in thought as I drove. Three murders. Boot-prints for a clue. Stolen priceless Prussian silverware. Two other victim's silverware missing. Arnie shooting at Yeti...bizarre! I yelled hello as we walked in. Arnie followed behind, cautiously, like an orphaned puppy-dog. I asked about the metal detector and was met with a word barrage the likes I hadn't heard in a long time. Guess Fritz hadn't bawled out anyone lately. 'Course, one never knows if he's serious. He was, and eventually got around to yelling "someone stole my brand new size ten Wolverine work boots off'n my front porch three weeks ago" and he'd "called the station but got told stolen boots weren't priority" and "was tired of waiting" and " 'bout time you got here. You gotta get them back. Right now!"

"I'd swear it was that damned Earl Peterson just down the road." Fritz pointed his crooked finger south toward the gravel road. "He said someone swiped his a while ago. I seen him yest'day with a brand new pair."

Interesting as that was, I wasn't about to do a shoe search. "Not a lot I can do about it, Fritz. How about that detector? Need to use it."

"Billy Conger borrowed it. Had it for a month now." Fritz followed that with a few more expletives, and pointed back down the dirt road again. "I'm gonna get that damn Peterson."

I warned Fritz about taking the law into his own hands, then Arnie and I loaded ourselves into the cruiser. We were overlooking something, and, crazy as it sounds, I couldn't convince myself we had a murdering Sasquatch roaming Omomqua County.

PING! The photos of the boot-print. There was something weird about them.

Back at headquarters, I laid three photos on my desk. I was right. I couldn't believe I missed it. "Arnie, what do you see?"

"Bloody boot-prints."

"Here, in front of the print. Hair would make marks like this, right?"

"But Jer, Billy Conger doesn't have any hair left...he's bald as a que ball. So's Fritz!"

I sighed. Sometimes Arnie just doesn't keep up. No, make that most time. The football injuries to his head were taking a toll. And he's still a young man. No wonder the Chief doesn't let him carry a loaded gun.

"B'sides, Jer, if Fritz's Wolverines were stolen, shouldn't we go after Earl Peterson?" Arnie argued. "Fritz said he had on a new pair. That's pretty conclusive."

"Maybe, Arn, but suspicion isn't enough to arrest." I picked up the photo and studied it. It DID look like hair but I refuse to believe Sasquatch could don work boots and murder. At least now I've got a couple of possible suspects: Billy Conger and Earl Petersen. Don't know about Fritz yet.

Someone confused us, and so far had done a good job. The bloody boot-prints definitely looked like Sasquatch had cut the toes out of a pair of Wolverines and squeezed in its feet, they'd extended 4 inches out of the boots. That just didn't fit, literally. These elusive creatures hadn't decided to come out of years of hiding to murder and pillage. And what in hell would they use silverware for anyway? It was time to do a little snooping around Earl's place.

Earl lived two miles south of Fritz's place on a narrow, rutted gravel road appropriately named "Dirt Road." He was a recluse. Pedaled his bicycle cart into town once a month to buy supplies, sell stuff he collected in the woods and his hand-made wind chimes. Most of it junk, but it sold like lottery tickets in the local Main Street grocery store/gas station/bowling alley. He'd do pencil drawings that could be of Bigfoot, or anything. Suspect Sasquatch footprint castings, locks of hair he claimed were real and metal chimes sold fast. I needed a closer look at the locks of hair.

No answer at Earl's, but the new Wolverine boots Fritz complained about were sitting on the front porch, last night's snow lingered in the boot's shadows. I motioned for Arnie to get out of the cruiser, but he shook his head no. I motioned again -- go around back, he wouldn't leave the car's safety. There's something strange about that boy. Guess I'll have a talk with the Chief about him when I'm done with this investigation. I decided to go alone. Peering through a dirty side window, I noticed a propane torch on the table, pliers, some strange misshapen pieces of metal and a couple small piles of...hair? Naw, more like well-worn wigs. Could this be Earl's genuine "Sasquatch" locks of hair? And the metal...silverware?

I hurried around to the back porch. The first thing that caught my eye was a large deep freezer. It was old. Big. Probably 160 cubic feet. Freezers, 'round here, are used to store deer and elk meat, but as far as I knew, Earl didn't hunt. Sensing danger, I drew my piece and approached the steps. All sorts of discarded junk littered the rotted decking -- burnt pots, broken chairs, a cracked wood-burning stove, busted snowshoes and a rusted red sled. I pulled plastic trash bags and empty restaurant sized bean cans off the freezer and opened it.

I'd been a skeptic all my life, but there it was, in all its glory...uhmmm, ex-glory. I stared directly into the face of a frozen ape-man. It was huge, filled the 8-foot long freezer. I could see where Earl'd cut off its hair, but the most shocking thing was its lack of feet. The creature's were missing. Hard to believe Arnie is correct, Sasquatch does exist. My hands started shaking as I remembered feeling something shadow Betsy and I. Quietly closing the lid, I made my way through the maze of clutter to the door. Pistol handy, I was going in.

If Earl were in the house, he could be sleeping...or waiting. Have I found the spinster killer? If he were capable of trapping and killing Sasquatch, then three old ladies wouldn't put up any kind of fight. Still, why would he murder them? Perhaps the hairy boot-print was Earl's attempt at throwing us off the trail. If he got away with those murders, I speculated he'd eventually skin Sasquatch and wear it for his next serial killing, the weather 'round here has been known to do strange things to the mind. The whole northwest would be in an uproar over a murdering ape-man...talk about a witch-hunt. But Earl wasn't that bright or he wouldn't allow himself to be caught this easily.

Shots rang out! Damn, Earl went out the front, shot Arnie. Wait, that sounded more like a service revolver. Arnie's got bullets? Where in hell'd he get 'em? He came flying around the side of the house, .38 snub-nose drawn, pointing towards the woods.

"Did you see it, Jerry? I shot it! It's limping. Come on. Come on."

Seeing Arnie in such a frantic state definitely caught me by surprise, but watching him run full speed was pro football poetry in motion. Despite his "supposed" bad knees, he was as graceful as the L.A Ram's Eric Dickerson, hurtling old couches, legless bathtubs and the sapling fence like fallen linebackers. I debated for a minute whether to enter the house, get Earl, or follow Arnie across the snow-covered yard. A loud growl, like the sound of a dying lion, bellowed from the brush and ended my indecision. I leaped from the porch and chased after Arnie.

PING! My head chimed again. This could be huge, tourism in our little town just got a boost. Sasquatch does exist around here, and there's one in Earl's freezer.

Arn waved his gun and yelled like an excited schoolgirl. I was about to shout "where'd you get bullets" when I saw it. Hairy, at least ten feet tall and close to 486 pounds, crashing through the brush like an out of control bulldozer. The swath it knocked down made a great path, but Arn was losing steam and I wasn't used to such a chase. The creature leapt over logs and boulders with ease, leaving us panting. Arn stopped and squeezed off several shots. I was out of breath. "Arnie, where'd you get bullets?"

"Get the Chief on the radio. Tell him to get the crew up to East Humptulips River, near Devil's Slide Lake."

That didn't sound like the Arnie Besmiller I knew. There's more to his story then anyone can imagine. I was awestruck. Arnie wasn't as lame-brained as he let on. I holstered my gun. That thing certainly wasn't Earl skeedaddling from the house. If he was still in there, Earl knew we were coming for him.

We stopped for a minute, listened to the dying sound of Bigfoot hurrying through trees.

"Man, it was fast," Arnie said, doubled over, hands on his knees. "I'm sure I hit it a couple of times."

I nodded, gasped into the microphone of my shoulder-mounted radio and relayed the situation to the Chief. I requested backup at Earls' and a search party mobilized for Devil's Slide Lake. It took some convincing, but the Chief finally agreed. I guess he deemed the information reliable coming from me and not Arnie. I concurred, signed off and yelled, "That was unreal Arn, sorry for doubting you all these years. Let's head back, gotta find Earl."

We moved toward the house. Breaking tree line, I saw another cruiser behind ours. I motioned the two officers around back. We were going to make a two-way breach. Arnie covered the front door, from behind the cruiser's fender. I knocked. "Earl, come on out."

"Earl's dead," a voice called out.

"Then you'd better step out with your arms raised and nothing in your hands," I yelled toward the house.

"OK, this first." An ancient double-barreled shotgun slid out of the ripped screen-door butt first. Fritz Hatchett eased out of the doorway, hands raised.

"Fritz? What the hell? Where's Earl?"

"Sasquatch got him," Fritz said, grinning ear to ear, holding his new Wolverine boots. "Tol' ya he stole my boots."

"You stealing them back?" I asked, knowing the answer.

"I don't steal nothin'," Fritz shouted. "I'm just taking them back where they rightfully belong." Squatting on the porch step, he pulled off his worn-out boots. "Got here just after you two did. Saw the ape-man go out the front door. It ripped Earl's head clean off." He slipped the new boots on and rubbed at fresh blood spotting them. "Guess ol' Sasquatch was jus' getting even. Earl killed his mate, ya know? Wondered why they were hanging around here so much."

"Hanging around?" I asked. "What do you mean?"

"Them Sasquatches been 'round Dirt Road for the last month. I hear 'em at night." Fritz finished tying his boots and stood. "Ya'll need to get in there and check out Earl, he's a mess."

"You stay here, Fritz. We got more talking to do."

I stepped inside. Arnie followed. Sure enough, Earl was deader than rock, lying what would have been face down if his head were still attached. "Where's his head?" I asked, following the bloody trail out the front door.

"Bigfoot," Arnie said, shaking his head. "Saw it, I hid behind the fender of the car. Didn't realize what it was at first, but it carried Earl's head...like a football."

"Call the coroner. Can't leave him like that."

Arnie picked up the phone in the living room. I heard him relay the report. I made my way to the kitchen wanting to investigate the metal pieces and wigs I saw. I needed to make sure our killer really was Earl.

After examining the objects on the table, I was convinced Earl was indeed the "Spinster Killer", but it appeared he had an accomplice. One piece of Maggie's missing silver had been fashioned into a wind chime, a hole drilled in the end with string ran through. Several pieces of the other two spinster's silver place-settings lay nearby. The chime was never finished. Slipped under one shiny butter knife was a note: Earl, quit using this for wind-chimes. This is real antique silver. Worth millions. I'll take it to Seattle-hock it. We'll share-80% for me and 25% for you. The handwriting looked familiar, but in the kitchen's dim light I couldn't tell if it was Billy Conger's, Fritz's, Earl's, the Chief's...or Arnie's.

I slipped the note into a plastic evidence bag and stuffed it in my pocket. I know...major Faux Pas, but someone close was an accomplice to a crime that extended beyond simple theft. I had no idea who to trust anymore and had to get to headquarters, compare handwriting samples.

Slipping past the medical examiner zipping Earl into a fresh black body bag, I stepped onto the sagging front porch. I handed Fritz my notebook, told him to write down his version of what just happened. I had two reasons. One, I needed a sample of his handwriting and two, I didn't think Fritz did it. He wouldn't know where to pawn silverware, and I don't think he's ever been out of Omomqua County, much less to all the way to Seattle. I do know this, someone is very nervous. I told Arnie to stay there and I beat feet for the station. The press, by now, had heard it on the scanner and would be all over the frozen Sasquatch. I shuddered thinking about questions I'd have to endure.

"Chief," I said over the radio, "pick up Billy Conger. Meet me at the station." I surmised that should throw suspicion on Billy. In the meantime, I'd stop at the courthouse, grab the handwritten copy of the Chief's acceptance speech and Arnie's hand-written entrance exam papers. One of these men killed three old ladies. I was determined to get him.

I needn't have worried about it. As I came out of the courthouse, the Chief called me on the radio. "Jerry? Jerry? Dammit-it-to-hell, get your ass back to Earl's. Hurry. Fritz called, said he'd been shot."

"Bring Conger." I slammed the mic onto the dash, the shifter into drive and left fourteen feet of black rubber marks in front of the courthouse.

Driving with my knees, I compared samples of Fritz's handwriting and the Chief's to the note. Neither was a match. In disgust, I flung them, hurled them toward the passenger side window, which, thank God was closed. The samples fluttered onto the floorboard. I noticed Arnie's notebook there. Straining to stay on the road, foot on the gas, hand on the wheel, I stretched to grab it. I opened it and put the yellowed note from Earl's next to a page. Perfect match. Damn, I should have known. He played for the Seahawks, has relatives in Seattle, including all three of his ex-wives. I hailed the Chief on the radio. "Send more backup to Earl's."

As I bounced the car into Earl's driveway, the distant sound of approaching sirens wailed. To my surprise, Arnie was still there. Sitting on the front stoop with his head in his hands like a redneck version of Auguste Rodin's "The Thinker." I opened the car door.

Approaching slowly, I noticed a revolver fill his hand. Had a feeling this wasn't going to end well. "Arn, why?" I asked, crouching behind the safety of the fencepost as he raised the pistol. He sobbed uncontrollably, quite a sight for a former football star.

"It just got out of hand," he yelled. "No one was supposed to get hurt...not even Earl."

The revolver crept higher.

"Earl never had much..." he said, "all's he wanted was a storefront to sell his wind chimes. I only wanted to help him...and get myself more money than this damned deputy job pays."

He waved the revolver in the air.

"Where's Fritz?" I asked.

"In the john."

"He OK?" I countered.

" 'Course he is, why?"

"Just wondering." I felt relieved. Apparently Fritz wanted us back here in a hurry before Arnie did something really stupid. "C'mon, Arn. Let's go."

"No! I'm not done explaining. Them old spinsters all had priceless silverware. Earl needed it," Arnie sobbed. "And my ex-wives are bleeding me dry. The first old lady was an accident. I swear."

I knew Arnie was playing his trump card, but chopping up Maggie wasn't an accident. It was frustration. One of us wasn't going to walk away from this. I stepped out from behind the fencepost hoping I wouldn't have to shoot.

"The second old lady wouldn't hand over her silver, she pulled a knife. The third I cut up after she called me Marshall, her hubby's name, gave me a big ol' sloppy kiss and told me she was getting even by poisoning my dinner...his dinner. Understand? She was a wacko...I got real scared."

I walked slowly toward Arnie. "It's over, Arn. Give me the gun."

"Can't," he said, sticking the barrel in his mouth. I wasn't close enough to do anything. I turned my face away just as he pulled the trigger.

Laughter erupted behind Arnie. I looked. Toilet paper unrolled and bounced down the porch steps. Arnie's gun hadn't gone off. He seemed bewildered. I was too.

Fritz chuckled. "Arnie laid his gun on the table when he phoned." Holding out his hand, open palm up. "I swiped his bullets."

Arnie was arraigned the next week on three counts of murder and we buried Earl. The television and news media barrage was like nothing our little town had seen before. Bigfoot hunters from around the world filled our lone hotel to capacity for weeks, the frozen Sasquatch disappeared and I'd heard the Smithsonian paid a cool $7 million for it and Earl's freezer. They denied it, of course, but sources tell me Sasquatch is in a vacuum-sealed glass case and a team of scientists pour over it inch by inch. I still haven't figured out who got the money, wasn't the town. And the feet are still missing.

Some weeks after, The Institute for Advanced Studies released a paper stating Sasquatch is a mutant branch of the evolutionary chain descending from Cro-Magnon and Lucy, but days after it appeared, that report was denied. I don't know what to believe. I know what I saw and no one, so far, has found Bigfoot's lair. There've been reports they're still around the area, sometimes seen at dusk...and I still wonder where Earl's head is. Late at night, I imagine them creatures in caves near Devil's Slide Lake dancing around a fire, holding a long branch with Earl's head prominently displayed atop it. Maybe I'll go hunting for it someday. I owe that to Earl.

Don't miss Roger's other books - available on Amazon, other fine booksellers and Kindle readers:

1.) **Bangin' Gears and Bustin' Heads.** Stories of high school car craziness way back in the early 1960's.

2.) **Fast Cars, 4-speeds and Fistfights.** Twenty-three episodes of high speed chaos, drag racing and high school shenanigans.

3.) **Recollections, Regrets and Random Acts.** Eleven "famous" and well known men in the hot rod hobby tell of past transgressions.

4.) **Accidents & Incidents (with assorted confessions).** Edge of your seat stories of car wrecks, cop chases, illegal drags and general car craziness.

5.) **Faded Thunder.** Stories of drag racing on Denver, ColoRODo streets, cruising the famous Scotchman drive-in and Denver's 16th Street.

6.) **Arsenal Code R.E.D.** Fiction set in Denver, ColoRODo. Two 15 year-olds steal into old the Stapleton International Airport control tower and are accused of causing an airliner crash into the Rocky Mountain Arsenal - home to millions of gallons of Sarin Nerve gas.

You may also want to visit www.RAJetter.com to purchase personally autographed copies of this book and to read other story excerpts.

CPSIA information can be obtained
at www.ICGtesting.com
Printed in the USA
FFOW05n2058011217